Caring
IN CRISIS

To

*Rachel
and
LC*

Caring in Crisis

Stories to Inspire and Guide School Leaders

Mark A. Smylie

Joseph F. Murphy

A SAGE Publishing Company

FOR INFORMATION:

Corwin
A SAGE Companyy
2455 Teller Road
Thousand Oaks, California 91320
(800) 233-9936
www.corwin.com

SAGE Publications Ltd.
1 Oliver's Yard
55 City Road
London EC1Y 1SP
United Kingdom

SAGE Publications India Pvt. Ltd.
B 1/I 1 Mohan Cooperative Industrial Area
Mathura Road, New Delhi 110 044
India

SAGE Publications Asia-Pacific Pte. Ltd.
18 Cross Street #10-10/11/12
China Square Central
Singapore 048423

ISBN: 9781071846988

President: Mike Soules
Associate Vice President and
   Editorial Director: Monica Eckman
Acquisitions Editor: Ariel Curry
Development Editor: Desirée A. Bartlett
Editorial Assistant: Caroline Timmings
Production Editor: Astha Jaiswal
Copy Editor: Pam Schroeder
Typesetter: Hurix Digital
Proofreader: Lawrence W. Baker
Cover Designer: Rose Storey
Marketing Manager: Morgan Fox

This book is printed on acid-free paper.

21 22 23 24 25 10 9 8 7 6 5 4 3 2 1

Contents

Coda

List of Illustrations

Preface

In the many years that we have worked in educational leadership and school improvement, we have come to believe that caring lies at the heart of schooling and promoting the learning and development of children. We have also come to believe that caring is an essential quality of school leadership. We are not alone in our thinking. Abundant evidence from research shows the importance of caring and support, along with high expectations and intellectual rigor, to the academic success of students. Educators know how essential it is for students' learning and well-being that they are in strong, trusting, caring relationships with adults and peers in and beyond school.

In 2020, we wrote a book exploring the concept of caring and its application to school leadership. That book, *Caring School Leadership* (Corwin), surveys writing and research from education, related academic fields and disciplines, and the human service professions. It identifies practices that school leaders might use to be caring in their relationships with students, cultivate their schools as caring communities, and foster caring in families and communities beyond the school.

Subsequently, we wrote a companion volume to that book titled *Stories of Caring School Leadership* (2021). In that book, we presented 100 true stories that illustrated concretely many of the practices of caring school leadership discussed in the first book. Those stories focused on the enactment of caring school leadership during what might be called "ordinary time" during the normal rhythms and flows of school life.

The present book of stories is also a companion to *Caring School Leadership*. Like the first book of stories, this book presents true stories that illustrate concretely many of the practices of caring school leadership. However, in the present book, we have assembled stories of caring school leadership during times of crisis. In *Caring School Leadership*, we wrote briefly about the importance of caring in crisis situations. And our first book of stories contained a few accounts that are set in crisis situations. Now, we give full attention to narratives that illustrate how caring school leadership can be practiced in times of crisis.

Purpose

The purpose of this book is to illuminate, instruct, and inspire. Through these stories, we portray key elements of caring school leadership practice during different crisis situations that schools may face. This book is not a primer on how to lead schools during a crisis, nor is it an inventory of practices that span the multiple functions of crisis leadership. Rather, this book shines a bright light on a crucial through line of crisis leadership—the importance of relationships and the imperative of caring. We introduce aspiring and practicing school leaders to practices that make crisis leadership humane and more caring. We encourage school leaders to reflect on their own practices and to challenge themselves to make caring a central quality of their leadership during crises and when crises subside.

The stories in this book are true. They describe events, actions, and interactions that occurred among real people in real places. Many stories are recounted by practicing and retired school leaders. Teachers, parents, and others also tell of their experiences with school leaders. Some accounts are autobiographical. Some describe caring leadership observed or experienced. We do not intend for the stories in this book to stand for generalizable evidence of the efficacy of caring school leadership, the importance of caring in crisis leadership, or any particular leadership practices. Instead, we see these stories as "existence proofs" of the possible.

Who Should Read This Book

This book was prepared for several audiences. One audience is aspiring and practicing school leaders. Another audience is those in higher education, professional associations, and other organizations that support the preparation and development of school leaders. We also believe that this book of stories can be useful to teachers and school staff, parents, community members, and others for developing caring leadership in schools and for defining expectations for their own school leaders.

We developed this book of stories as a resource for individual principals and other school leaders to read and reflect upon. It can be a basis for stimulating discussion about caring within school leader preparation and development programs. It can be helpful as schools prepare for crises and as they respond to and recover from them. We also see the book as a resource for administrative leaders and teachers to consider together to develop strong and effective school leadership and improve schools for students. Several specific ways that this book can be used are presented at the end of this preface.

You will find little of our own analysis and interpretation of the stories herein. We want the stories to speak for themselves. We want you to hear the storytellers' voices, not ours. You are encouraged to reflect upon these narratives and discuss them with others. And you are encouraged to analyze them, give them your own meaning, and apply them to your own situations. We provide a guide to help you engage the stories in these ways.

Our Starting Point

This book proceeds from our belief in the vital importance of caring in schools and in school leadership and in our belief in the power and legitimacy of stories for the development and promotion of leadership practice. As writers from psychiatrist Robert Coles to organization and management scholar Henry Mintzberg observe[1], stories can call us to consider what is right and true. Stories play an increasingly important role in programs of educational leadership preparation and development. Teaching cases are widely promoted as an effective means of helping aspiring school leaders understand the nature of their work, examine their own practice, and develop new ways to exercise leadership.

Stories play an important role in practicing school leaders' learning. Oral storytelling is a primary means of on-the-job information sharing and knowledge development. So too are accounts of programs and practices told through the pages of professional magazines. Stories are an important means of vicarious learning for school leaders. Sometimes ignored by academic scholars who favor more systematically developed quantitative evidence to guide practice, such narratives can be powerful sources of new knowledge, understanding, legitimation, and motivation for practicing school leaders.

The Literature

To introduce the stories in this book, we draw on several bodies of scholarly and professional literature. We look to literature on crisis leadership and management from the fields of business and management, public administration, public health, social and psychological services, and education.

---

[1] Coles (1989), Mintzberg (2019).

Because our focus is on schools and school leadership, we concentrate on aspects of this literature that focus on organizations and organizational leadership.

We also look to scholarly and professional literature on caring and caring leadership. Here too we draw from several disciplines and fields of study including education, philosophy, ethics, sociology, political science, business and management, and organizational studies. We draw from literature of other human service professions that recognize the importance of caring in organizational contexts including health care and social-services administration, nursing and medicine, and the ministry.

Our purpose is not to present an in-depth treatment of this literature. Our focus is on stories and the lived experiences of crises and caring in school leadership. We use general insights from the literature to make the case for caring in crisis leadership and to frame the stories for reading and reflection. We encourage readers who wish to learn more about caring and crisis leadership and management to refer to our bibliography and our book *Caring School Leadership*.

Elicitation and Selection of Stories

We elicited stories for this book between November 2020 and early January 2021. We reached out to contributors to our book *Stories of Caring School Leadership* to see if they had stories to tell about caring school leadership during times of crisis. We activated our networks of practicing and retired educators. And we contacted current and former students who are currently working in schools. We sought stories from principals, associate principals, heads of school, department chairs, teachers, superintendents, staff, and others who interact with principals, heads, and other school leaders. We did not elicit stories from students, nor did we engage in systematic sampling. Nevertheless, we ended up with an archive of stories that come from a wide range of schools across many settings.

We were general in what we asked of our storytellers. We wanted them to determine for themselves what situations constituted crises for their schools. However, we wanted them to focus on situations that rose above and beyond problems and challenges that are associated with normal life in schools and to address situations that posed out-of-the-ordinary collective threat, difficulty, risk, or harm. While leaving the door open to any situation our storytellers considered a crisis, we noted different types of crises about which they could write.

Similarly, we wanted to give our storytellers latitude to determine what leadership actions and interactions they considered caring. We provided only a general sense of what we meant by caring school leadership—working for the betterment of others, supporting others and addressing their needs and problems, and promoting their general success and well-being. We gave our storytellers room to write about caring in school leaders' relationships with individuals and groups of students, teachers, and staff; in the school as a community for students, teachers, and staff; and beyond the school in relation to families and neighborhoods.

We told our storytellers that they could write about their own experiences as school leaders. They could share stories about other school leaders. They could write in first or third person, and they could use dialog they remembered. Our only stipulation was that the events they wrote about had to have actually happened. We told our storytellers that they did not have to tell positive stories of caring. They were encouraged to share stories of problematic caring or caring gone wrong. We did not want this book to consist only of feel-good or happy stories. Problematic and negative stories can be instructive too.

From our efforts, we received nearly 100 stories. From this number, we selected 40 stories for this book. These stories illustrate important ways in which caring school leadership is practiced during different crisis situations. They are *not* a comprehensive representation of the untold number of ways that school leaders can be caring during crisis. They are but a sampling and are what our storytellers chose to share with us. We strongly suggest that as you read and reflect upon these stories, you also think beyond them to consider other ways that the central elements of caring can manifest themselves in school leadership during crises.

The stories we selected for this book represent a number of different crisis situations. There are stories about the overwhelming, shared public health crisis—the COVID-19 pandemic. There are also stories of natural disasters; violence and social unrest; hunger, homelessness, and unemployment; mental health crises; sexual abuse; and personal crises that became matters for school communities. We favored accounts of crises that originate outside the school rather than crises of schools' or school districts' own making (e.g., performance failures). Crises of internal origin are important to understand and address, but examining them is beyond the scope of this volume. In addition, we selected narratives from different types of schools and settings. You will read stories from preschools, elementary schools, middle schools, and high schools. You will read stories from urban, suburban, small-town, and rural schools and communities. And you will read stories from public, independent, and religious schools.

The stories in this book come from across the country. Not surprisingly, most come from regions in which we live and work. About 40 percent of the stories are from the Midwest, 37 percent are from the South and Southeast, and 23 percent are from the East and West Coasts, the Southwest, and the North and Northeast. They come from 31 different school districts or municipalities from Massachusetts to California, from Minnesota to Louisiana, and many points in between. Approximately 57 percent of stories come from urban settings, 30 percent from suburban settings, and 13 percent from small-town and rural settings.

Our stories are published with the permission of their authors, who are recognized by name in the book's acknowledgments. To protect privacy, we do not associate our storytellers' names or school names with the stories themselves. We also removed or altered information that might serve to identify individuals or places. For the few stories that are adapted from published sources, complete removal of identifying information was not possible. To illustrate the variety of schools and locales from which these stories come, we have noted beneath each story title the role of the storyteller (e.g., principal, teacher, parent), the locale (e.g., small town, rural, suburban, urban), and grade level of the school (e.g., elementary, middle, high school).

Student Artwork

Throughout this book you will find pieces of student artwork on caring and crisis. This artwork comes from several sources. A middle school teacher in Nashville, Tennessee, and a high school teacher in Richmond, Virginia, asked students in their classes to produce drawings for our project. Using a simple prompt that we supplied, they asked students to draw a picture to show how it felt to be cared for when they faced a situation that made them feel uncertain, threatened, or afraid. They could refer in their drawings to a specific event or render an image of a general feeling. The teacher from Richmond also gave us access to artwork previously produced in her school's art classes. From the associate head of a secondary school in Potomac, Maryland, we received drawings produced by students as part of projects completed in their art classes. Finally, Mark Smylie invited children and youth in his neighborhood of Oak Park, Illinois, to draw for the project.

We selected 14 of the drawings we received to illustrate students' views of caring in times of crisis. Our contributing artists come from PreK through 12th grade. Their drawings can be considered "graphic stories" of how children and youth perceive caring in crisis. The names of our artists and their grade levels are shown beneath their drawings as are the titles we gave to each. Each drawing is published with parent permission.

Organization

We organized this book as a companion to our books *Caring School Leadership* and *Stories of Caring School Leadership*. Although each book stands on its own and can be read independently, we wanted to make it easy for our audiences to read across all three volumes. To this end, we assembled this book to align with both of our earlier works.

The first section of the book lays the groundwork for our stories. We begin with an **Introduction** that brings forward our concept of caring school leadership developed and illustrated in the first two books, and we apply this concept to crisis leadership and management. We reintroduce key elements and arenas of caring school leadership practice from the first two books and apply them to school leadership during times of crisis.

Following this Introduction, we provide a short **Guide for Engaging the Stories**. The guide provides an overview of practices that are explored in *Caring School Leadership* and are illustrated by the stories in this book. The guide also provides questions for reflection and discussion. We crafted these questions so that they can be adapted to individual reading and reflection, group discussion, leader preparation and development, and joint administrator–staff work in schools. They are designed to deepen understanding of caring, its key elements, and how caring may function in crisis situations. Also, they are designed to promote reflection upon and application of practices in the stories to readers' own situations. These questions ask readers to compare their own assumptions, biases, and practices with those reflected in the stories. They ask readers to consider context and how stories might play out similarly or differently in their own situations. They ask readers how they might answer the question "What would you do?" if presented with similar crises. Our questions were inspired by authors and teachers.[1] We favored questions that guide readers toward understanding and meaning and that push them toward personal and professional reflection.

The second section of the book presents **The Stories**. The stories focus on two of the three arenas of caring school leadership practice as described in *Caring School Leadership*. These arenas are school leaders' interpersonal relationships with students, teachers, and staff and the context of the school as a community. Stories of practice in the third arena of caring school leadership—families and neighborhoods beyond the school—are beyond the scope of this book. For stories of caring school leadership in families and neighborhoods beyond the school, see *Stories of Caring School Leadership*.

---

[1] For example, Donaldson (2006) and Garmston (2019).

The purpose of the stories in this book is to illuminate key aspects of caring leadership in crisis situations and how caring manifests itself therein. Through examples of how caring school leadership is practiced across different crisis situations, we may better understand the importance of caring in crisis leadership, and we can discern important cross-cutting insights and lessons for practice.

Many of the stories in this volume provide direct lessons on the nature and function of caring in school leadership during times of crisis. Some stories lend themselves to differing interpretations. Some you will find inspiring and uplifting. Others you may find troubling and disquieting. You may agree or disagree with the thinking and actions of the school leader. Yet, all these stories can be sources of learning.

Our stories are presented in no particular order. Stories of different crisis situations are mixed together as are stories of caring in the interpersonal and organizational arenas of practice. Mixed together are stories of elementary, middle, and high schools and stories of public, independent, and religious schools.

As mentioned earlier, we make no systematic effort to analyze, interpret, or convey the meaning we might attribute these stories. However, in the third section of the book, we offer a short reflection, or **Coda**, on the importance of caring in school leadership during times of crisis and implications for caring school leadership when crises subside. We also discuss the critical question: "Who cares for the caring school leader?"

How to Use This Book

There are many ways that you can use this book. You can use it for independent reading and reflection. You can read and think about the stories, beginning with the first one and moving through the book to the last. Or you can flip through, skipping around, reading those stories that are of particular interest to you. You can read this book by yourself, considering a story or two every day as a centering activity, or you can form or join a group of school leaders to read and discuss these accounts together.

This book can be used as a resource for programs that prepare aspiring school leaders for service and as a resource for programs of professional development for practicing school leaders. It can serve as case material for instructors and groups of learners to read, analyze, and apply to their own situations and practice. We strongly recommend working with these stories in group settings.

The stories in this book can serve as a foundation for a variety of learning activities in school leader preparation and development. They can be used as examples of practice to be reflected upon, analyzed, discussed, and compared to learners' own thinking and practice. These stories can become the basis of role-playing, whereby learners assume the roles of persons in the stories and act out the story line as written or as key facts of the story might be changed. Learners can create and improvise extensions of stories, imagining, acting, and discussing what might come next and why. Moreover, these narratives can be used to help aspiring and practicing school leaders tell their own stories about particular crisis situations. Composing one's own stories and conveying them to others can help learners organize their thoughts, reflect upon their own assumptions and actions, and raise important issues. Sharing stories can stimulate collaborative analysis and joint problem-solving. There are many other learning activities that might spring from this book of stories.

Crisis preparation and prevention are important; so too is developing the human relationships, the trust, and the capacity for caring that might help prevent particular types of crises and become invaluable resources for encountering and recovering from them.

Last but not least, this book of stories can be used by practicing leaders working in schools with faculty, staff, parents, and students. You can use this book to help inform work to prepare your school community for crises and to lead your school when crises arise. Much of the guidance for crisis prevention and preparation now available to schools focuses on operational matters, on ways to detect potential crises, and on ways to develop particular routines and protocols and train people to use them. Although these aspects of crisis preparation and prevention are important, so too is developing the human relationships, the trust, and the capacity for caring that might help prevent particular types of crises and become invaluable resources for encountering and recovering from crises that do occur. We hope that this book will help schools become the schools before a crisis that they would want to be when a crisis comes.

For principals and other school leaders who wish to strengthen caring in their districts, schools, and classrooms, this book can become a source of learning for all. These stories provide vivid examples of caring school communities that schools may wish to cultivate. They provide examples for developing caring school leadership among teachers as well as administrators. And, they can help schools collectively develop shared expectations for caring in administrative and teacher leadership alike. We envision these stories being used in teacher professional development workshops, in professional communities, and in schoolwide improvement sessions. We see these stories used to remind administrators and teachers of the aims, virtues, and mindsets of caring and the importance to students of strong, trusting interpersonal relationships and caring school communities. Indeed, we imagine a principal starting each faculty meeting with a story of caring to focus the work of the school around a core value. We imagine these stories serving as a springboard for administrators and staff to tell their own stories to stimulate expanded and deeper caring.

We hope that you find these stories enjoyable to read, challenging, and reaffirming of the importance of caring in school leadership during crisis situations. We hope that you find them illuminating, instructive, and inspirational for your practice. And, we hope that you will be convinced to continue, even amplify, the caring that emerges when crises come after those crises subside.

Acknowledgments

This book is inspired by scores of practicing educators with whom we have worked in districts and schools and in our classrooms. It is also inspired by the PreK–12 students who we see prosper in schools when they are both challenged and cared for.

We are deeply grateful to the practicing and retired educators and others who contributed stories to this book. We are indebted to the following persons, listed alphabetically, who shared their stories with us and gave us permission to share them with you:

John Borrero, Matthew Dodd Campbell, Kristin Cantrell, Ryan Cantrell, Ed Condon, Tom Conroy, Don Davis, Lora Dever, Jonathan Ellwanger, Dwayne Evans, Lauren Gage, Kevin Gallick, Jeff Greenfield, Andrew Harris, Steven Henn, Jenny Escamilla Howell, Brandon Hubbard-Heitz, Lauren Huddleston, Regan Humphrey, Carol Kampa, Amanda Klein-Cox, Peggy Korellis, Jeana Leitz, Eliza McGehee, Cathy McGehee, Martin McGreal, Sarah McIlroy, Ryan McLaughlin, Ben Owens, Emily Palmer, Alice Phillips, Erin Roche, Maisha Rounds, Zach Swope, Allison Tingwall, Lisa Vardi, Vanessa Williams-Johnson, Jackie Wilson, Michele Zurakowsky

We thank a number of people who helped us find storytellers for this book. Special appreciation is extended to Cynthia Barron, Milena Batanova, Ariel Curry, Jon Eckert, Jonathan Ellwanger, Jeff Ikler, Glenn Manning, Ben Owens, and Patrick Schuermann.

We thank Ari Frede, Lauren Gage, Eliza McGehee, Lisa Vardi, and the parents of Forest Avenue and surrounds for their invaluable assistance to gather student artwork for this book. Our student artists are recognized by name in the List of Illustrations and where their drawings appear throughout the book. We are grateful to them for sharing their thoughts and emotions through their art.

We thank Anna Caldwell for preparing several of these several drawings for publication. Personal appreciation is extended to Sallie Smylie for her keen eye, critical perspective, patience and good humor, and sense of the whole puzzle we were trying to assemble we were focused on individual pieces.

We thank Ariel Curry, Desirée Bartlett, Astha Jaiswal, and Corwin for help to bring this book to life.

Finally, we are ever so grateful to our families for their love, caring, and support.

About the Authors

Mark A. Smylie is professor of education emeritus in the Department of Educational Policy Studies at the University of Illinois at Chicago and visiting professor in the Department of Leadership, Policy, and Organizations at Peabody College, Vanderbilt University. Before his work in higher education, Smylie was a high school social studies teacher. Smylie served as secretary-treasurer of the National Society for the Study of Education and as a director of the Consortium on Chicago School Research at the University of Chicago. Smylie has worked with schools, school districts, and school administrator and teacher professional associations through joint projects, advising, and school leader development activities. He has served on advisory boards of numerous regional and national professional and policy organizations concerned with education generally and leadership in particular. Smylie's research focuses on school organization, leadership, and change.

Joseph F. Murphy is professor of education emeritus and the former Frank W. Mayborn Chair of Education in the Department of Leadership, Policy, and Organizations at Peabody College of Education at Vanderbilt University. He has also been a faculty member at the University of Illinois at Urbana-Champaign and The Ohio State University, where he was William Ray Flesher Professor of Education. In the public schools, Murphy has served as an administrator at the school, district, and state levels, including an appointment as the executive assistant to the chief deputy superintendent of public instruction in California. He was the founding president of the Ohio Principals Leadership Academy. Murphy's work is in the area of school improvement with special emphasis on leadership and policy.

Introduction: Crises and Caring School Leadership

Crisis Comes

Crisis has become a prominent condition of contemporary organizational life.[2] No organization is immune. It is not a question of whether a crisis will strike an organization but only a matter of when, how, what form it will take, and who and how many people will be affected.

It follows that all organizational leaders can count on facing some kind of crisis at some point in their careers.[3] Most will face multiple crises. Sometimes crises will come one at a time and will be spread far apart. Sometimes they will come in rapid succession, even simultaneously. Thus, every leader will at some point become a crisis leader.

Most crises do not announce their coming. Sometimes they can be anticipated, but many times they cannot. Regardless, crises do not wait until organizations are prepared for them. Nor do they wait for leaders to develop the ability to guide their organizations through them effectively. Joshua Sharfstein of the Johns Hopkins Bloomberg School of Public Health makes the wry observation: "There's a name for the day when crises hit public health agencies: Monday. Also, Tuesday, Wednesday, Thursday, Friday, Saturday, and Sunday."[4]

Similar observations have been made about crises and schools. Increasingly, schools across the globe have had to respond to traumatic incidents affecting them and their surrounding communities.[5] The frequency and severity of some types of crisis have increased. No matter what they do to prevent and prepare for them, schools cannot avoid completely unwanted disturbances and intrusions of crisis.[6] They cannot avoid completely the prospects of negative consequences for their operations and outcomes and for the safety and well-being of students, teachers, and staff.[7]

How school leaders lead during crises is of critical importance to how schools will fare as a result of them. In this introduction we explore caring as a critical quality of crisis leadership. We argue that caring is not a function apart from other functions of crisis leadership. Rather, it is the matter, manner, and motivation of those functions and how they are performed. This is the same as understanding caring to be a quality of all leadership actions and interactions and of any school leadership function.

We begin this introduction examining the meaning of crisis in organizations generally and in schools in particular. We turn to discuss the core functions of crisis leadership and the critical "through line" of human relationships and caring in the performance of those functions. This discussion takes us to examine the meaning and expression of caring in school leadership and to a model of caring school leadership. We conclude this introduction by applying this model to school leadership in times of crisis.

The Meaning of Crisis

The word *crisis* comes from the Greek word *krisis*, which means turning point or decisive point in the progression of something. Following this original meaning, Gene Klann of the Center for Creative Leadership considers crisis a "turning point in the affairs of an individual or an organization."[8]

---

[2] Gigliotti (2020), Klann (2003).
[3] Klann (2003).
[4] Sharfstein (2018, p. 59).
[5] MacNeil and Topping (2007).
[6] Thompson (2004).
[7] Mutch (2015).
[8] Klann (2003, p. 4).

Such turning points are significant because they may be critical to the future of that individual or organization.

> **Crisis:** a turning point in the affairs of an individual or an organization, potentially critical to the future of that individual or organization.

Most definitions of crisis describe it as a time of intense difficulty or danger, a time when a hard or consequential decision must be made, even a time when the survival of a person or an organization is at stake. For example, Arjen Boin and his colleagues describe crisis as "a serious threat to the basic structures or the fundamental values and norms of a system, which under time pressure and highly certain circumstances necessitates making vital decisions."[9] Christine Pearson and Ian Mitroff define crisis as "an incident or event [that poses] a threat to the organization's reputation and viability."[10] And Erika James and Lynn Wooten see crisis as "a rare and significant situation that has the potential to . . . bring about highly undesirable outcomes . . . therefore, requiring immediate corrective action."[11]

Education scholars offer similar definitions of crises in schools. Mary Margaret Kerr and Garry King define a school crisis as an event or condition that affects a school, causing individuals to experience fear, helplessness, shock, or horror.[12] To them, a school crisis requires extraordinary actions to restore a sense of psychological and physical security. Similarly, Wilson MacNeil and Keith Topping describe school crises as "sudden, unexpected events that have an emergency quality and have the potential to impact the whole school community."[13] To MacNeil and Topping a school crisis might be any situation far outside the normal experience by staff or students that causes unusually strong emotional reactions that interfere with their ability to perform. And to Matthew Pepper and his colleagues, a school crisis is "an event or a series of events that threaten a school's core values or foundational practices."[14]

Across these definitions are several factors that distinguish crises from other situations, such as routine problems and challenges, even those that pose difficulty and discomfort. Indeed, not every problem, not every piece of "unfortunate or unpleasant business" rises to the level of a crisis.[15] According to Christine Pearson and her colleagues, crises "hyper-extend" the capabilities of the organization: "They tug high-impact organizational decisions and actions into uncharted waters."[16] Crises pose serious threats in real time and create substantial uncertainty and stress. They can be chaotic and confusing. They can cause severe disruption. And they have the potential to overwhelm usual coping mechanisms and require immediate response.

Crises can originate inside or outside a school, and they can be unpredictable or foreseen.[17] They may arrive in a flash or result from a slow boil.[18] Their sources can be natural or man-made.[19] Crises can occur at the personal, organizational, or community level.[20] A crisis that originates at one level may have important implications for other levels. For example, a crisis that occurs in a community may

[9] Boin et al. (2005, p. 3).
[10] Pearson and Mitroff (1993, p. 49).
[11] James and Wooten, 2010, p. 5).
[12] Kerr and King (2019, p. 3).
[13] MacNeil and Topping (2007, p. 66).
[14] Pepper et al. (2010, p. 6).
[15] James and Wooten (2004, p. 5).
[16] Pearson et al. (1997, p. 52).
[17] Mitroff et al. (1988), Pepper et al. (2010).
[18] James and Wooten (2004).
[19] Raphael (1986).
[20] Dückers (2017).

have important implications for schools therein. A personal crisis may have significant implications for the school as a whole. A relatively small, manageable crisis may blossom into a large, unmanageable one for numerous reasons, including lack of preparedness or inadequate initial response. Indeed, James and Wooten observe that it is not the crisis itself that necessarily poses the greatest threat but the handling of the crisis.[21]

It is equally important to understand that what makes a situation a crisis is more than calling it one or an objective assessment of the situation. Crisis has a socially constructed meaning. It involves a subjective understanding of threat and risk. At the heart of a crisis is a perception of vulnerability and the ability to respond.[22] This phenomenological dimension of crisis is shaped by one's role and responsibility, one's history with crisis-like situations, and one's perceived ability to deal with the conditions present.[23] It is also shaped by the meanings constructed by and with others.

Why does this matter? Both facts and subjective meanings will influence how an organization—a school—anticipates and prepares for crisis, engages and contains crisis, and recovers and learns from crisis. Together, they will shape the nature and function of what is called crisis leadership. The importance of the subjective understanding of crisis drove our approach to story elicitation and our decision not to impose our own definition of crisis on our storytellers.

Crisis Leadership and the Through Line of Caring

Crisis leadership is a special case of general leadership. What makes it a special case are particular functions that are different from or variations of the functions that organizational leaders typically perform.[24] These functions are critical to navigating crisis. They include recognizing emerging threats, initiating efforts to mitigate them and deal with their consequences, and once the acute period of crisis has passed, reestablishing a sense of normalcy and learning from the experience. We will say more about these functions shortly.

Crisis Management and Crisis Leadership

Crisis management: an approach that focuses on operational and managerial domains of leadership work performed before, during, and after a crisis.

A distinction is sometimes drawn between crisis management and crisis leadership. Both point to important aspects of dealing effectively with a crisis. Crisis management focuses on operational and managerial domains of leadership work performed before, during, and after a crisis. These include but are not limited to crisis planning, conducting training and drills, forming crisis teams, assigning specific roles to be performed during a crisis situation, and managing communications and public relations. This work is necessary but insufficient to guide organizations through a crisis successfully.

---

[21] James and Wooten (2004, p. 8).
[22] Sharfstein (2018, p. 5).
[23] Gigliotti (2020).
[24] Klann (2003), Mutch (2015).

> **Crisis leadership:** an approach maintaining a vision of what was, what is, and what could be; staying attuned to the big picture; promoting meaning and sensemaking; sustaining organizational culture and social relationships; and seeking opportunities that may result from crisis.

Crisis leadership is a broader construct that includes these operational and managerial domains and adds to them a crucial executive domain.[25] The executive domain includes, among other things, maintaining a vision of what was, what is, and what could be; staying attuned to the big picture of crisis situations; promoting meaning and sensemaking; sustaining organizational culture and social relationships; and seeking opportunities for the organization that may result from crisis. We prefer the broader, more inclusive construct of crisis leadership to crisis management. Our preference aligns with findings of research that leaders who successfully recover from crisis and maintain the reputations of their organizations understand the importance of crisis management and do it well. At the same time, they say that management is insufficient, that the broader, executive function of crisis leadership work is also critically important.

Phases of Crisis Leadership

Crisis leadership is often described according to phases or stages of crisis. At its simplest, crisis leadership can be thought of in terms of an "emergency phase," when the task is to stabilize the situation and buy time, and an "adaptive phase," when the underlying causes of the crisis are addressed and capacity to thrive in a new reality are developed.[26] More common is to think about crisis leadership in terms of four or five phases. The PPRR Model focuses on phases of prevention, preparation, response, and recovery.[27] This model was adopted and slightly modified by the U.S. Department of Education in 2013.

Five-phase models elaborate these phases and are more specific about the work associated with each. To illustrate, we look across two similar models developed by Ian Mitroff and his colleagues[28] and Erika James and Lynn Wooten and find the following.[29]

1. *Signal detection* involves anticipating crisis and spotting red flags or warning signals that something is wrong.

2. *Preparation and prevention* include measures to fend off crisis and to ready direct responses when crisis comes. Preparation can include probing one's organization for weaknesses, identifying organizational resources that might be drawn upon, assigning roles and responsibilities that will need to be performed, and preparing people for those roles and responsibilities. Often preparation involves developing structures, such as crisis teams, to manage crisis response.

3. *Containment and damage control* focus on direct response to a crisis when it strikes. This phase may include actions to isolate and absorb the shock of the crisis, cope with it, and limit negative impact.

4. *Recovery* is the work of short- and long-term healing and repair, and it involves steps to return to normalcy.

---

[25] James and Wooten (2004).
[26] Heifetz et al.(2020).
[27] MacNeil and Topping (2007).
[28] Mitroff et al. (1988), Pearson and Mitroff (1993).
[29] James and Wooten (2010).

5. *Reflection and learning* involve explicit efforts to understand the underlying causes of the crisis and to assess the implementation and effectiveness of the response. Done well, this phase is crucial for improving each of the first four phases for future crises, especially preparation and prevention. This phase can also be an effective springboard to promoting more general improvement to organizational performance and outcomes.

The Work of Crisis Leadership

Leading during crisis requires, as Christine Pearson and her colleagues observe, a "coordinated, full-blown multifunctional effort."[30] This effort involves operational, managerial, and executive domains of leadership we highlighted earlier. Crisis leadership is context-specific work. Its effectiveness is determined by its relevance to the "situational contingencies" of a particular organization and its community.[31] Moreover, although effective crisis leadership is "planful," it is also "emergent" and "auto-adaptive." That is, it adjusts to fit the ever-changing crisis situation and context.[32]

Now, we examine 10 specific functions that constitute the work of crisis leadership. Most of these functions apply across different phases of crisis leadership. A number have managerial as well as executive dimensions. As such, we do not identify them with specific phases or domains. We encourage you to consider the managerial and executive aspects of each as well as how different functions might apply to different phases of crisis leadership.

10 Functions of Crisis Leadership

1. Reinforcing the organization's mission and core values and setting a vision and priorities for the future

2. Promoting meaning and sensemaking

3. Providing assurance, inspiring confidence, and creating stability

4. Communicating

5. Sharing leadership and decision-making

6. Coordinating operations and management

7. Acquiring and allocating resources

8. Learning from crisis

9. Improving into the future

10. Tending to people and to relationships

1. *Reinforcing the organization's mission and core values and setting a vision and priorities for the future.* Effective crisis leaders reinforce the core purposes and values of the organization for its members, constituents, and stakeholders. This provides an important source of stability amid the uncertainty and threat of crisis. Effective crisis leaders also facilitate a shared vision for what is desired throughout and following a crisis.[33]

---

[30] Pearson et al. (1997, p. 52).
[31] Quarantelli (1998, p. 375).
[32] Anderson (2018, p. 50), Comfort (2007, p. 195).
[33] Anderson (2018).

Such a vision sets an expectation that can unify an organization emotionally, operationally, and politically. And it can promote common understanding that enables coordinated action. Reanchoring on organizational mission and core values, and projecting a vision for moving forward, lays the foundation for short- and long-term priorities that set strategic direction when responding to a crisis and working to recover and learn from it.

2. *Promoting meaning and sensemaking.* Effective crisis leadership aims to promote collective understanding of a crisis and help people make meaning of it in ways that bring authentic hope, confidence, and resilience.[34] A shared base of knowledge and understanding—a "common operating picture"—is crucial for collective action in extreme circumstances.[35] It is important to ground meaning making of a crisis in the organization's mission, vision, core values, and priorities.

3. *Providing assurance, inspiring confidence, and creating stability.* Crises can disrupt, disorient, and damage. They can introduce danger, upheaval, and debilitating ambiguity and uncertainty. A key function of crisis leadership is to provide assurance and inspire confidence that the organization is taking ownership of the situation as much as possible, not allowing the situation to take ownership of the organization.[36] How leaders demonstrate responsibility in a crisis, how they explain problems, and how they collaborate and make key decisions with others can go far to inspire confidence and credibility. Leaders can promote assurance by modeling coping, encouraging the expression of feelings, and affirming emotional responses. Leaders can promote stability through regular communication, reasserting routines and rituals, elevating symbols that convey shared meaning, and reinforcing the organization's mission and core values.

4. *Communicating.* Keeping people informed about a crisis, what is being done to address it, and the progress being made are crucial to crisis leadership. Effective communication is vital to developing a common understanding, conveying important information for action, and promoting credibility and trust. A formal communication strategy is essential to any organization before, during, and after a crisis situation. Because crises can disrupt normal communication channels, creative use of unconventional means of communication may be necessary. Effective communication allows leaders to maintain quality control over the flow of information within and outside the organization.[37] It allows leaders not only to share information but to form a persuasive narrative that explains what happened, the consequences, how the situation can be resolved, and who can be relied upon to resolve it.[38] The amount of communication is less important than the ability to develop the "cognition" of risk and response.[39] Personal communication involving humble inquiry[40] and strategic listening[41] is crucial. Hallmarks of effective crisis communication include clarity, accuracy, consistency, honesty, and authenticity. It is important to tell it straight but also shape the message considering how it will be received. Leaders can communicate a great deal about their seriousness and sincerity by being visible and physically, mindfully, and emotionally present. They should be seen and heard. Being present can convey empathy and concern

---

[34] Gigliotti (2020), Teo et al. (2017).
[35] Comfort (2007).
[36] Waldron and Wetherbe (2020).
[37] Pepper et al. (2010).
[38] Sharfstein (2018).
[39] Comfort (2007).
[40] Schein (2013).
[41] Tate and Dunklee (2005).

and build trust and confidence in ways that written words cannot.

5. ***Sharing leadership and decision-making.*** Too often, leaders assume that centralized control and decision-making must be imposed to confront the disruption and

uncertainty of crisis. Just the opposite may be needed. Proactively affording people affected by crisis more influence and control may reduce feelings of insecurity and helplessness and increase a sense of control. Making sure that people have meaningful things to do can calm anxiety, help restore order, and promote a sense of agency.[42] Moreover, tapping multiple points of view can lead to better decision quality. It is important to expand influence across what happens during a crisis and over how and when these things happen.[43] Related to sharing leadership and decision-making is managing politics. Effective crisis leaders manage the politics within their own organizations. They encourage a shift from adversarial to more consensual politics where the pursuit of collective interests replaces the pursuit of self and group interests. Leaders should look beneath a particular political issue to understand the interests, fears, aspirations, and loyalties that have formed around it.[44] Effective crisis leaders also work with external political leadership, such as that in the larger community. External political leadership may be a crucial source of support, providing moral and legal authority and political leverage to enact potentially controversial decisions and to secure needed resources.[45]

6. ***Coordinating operations and management.*** This function includes making sure that there is a strong management system in place before crisis comes and that the components of this system are coherent, well coordinated, and flexible enough to adapt to crisis situations. Effective crisis leaders make sure that there are clear protocols and assignments, sufficient resources, and opportunities for management and operations personnel to raise questions, anticipate problems, share information, suggest new solutions, and make decisions themselves.[46]

7. ***Acquiring and allocating resources.*** Crises may call on leaders to acquire additional resources and allocate them to meet particular needs. These may include fiscal, material, and technological resources. They may also include space, time, and human resources, especially human service professionals and other sources of service and expertise. Acquiring such resources may depend on entrepreneurial acumen. Importantly, effective crisis leaders ensure that resources flow to priority areas.[47] Their allocation and use need to be monitored and adjusted as conditions change. Importantly, leaders will need to employ the social resources of the organization—interpersonal relationships, trust, support, and mutual commitment.

8. ***Learning from crisis.*** Effective crisis leaders take steps to understand the experience of crisis and learn what might be done better in the future.[48] Leaders should reflect and engage

---

[42] Sharfstein (2018).
[43] Sutton (2020).
[44] Heifetz et al. (2020).
[45] Kahn (2020).
[46] Sharfstein (2018).
[47] Pepper et al. (2010).
[48] O'Connor and Takahashi (2014).

others throughout the organization in post-mortem activities to assess what aspects of anticipation, response, and recovery were successful or unsuccessful.[49] Such learning can be directed toward improved crisis planning and prevention as well as toward developing more effective strategies for response and recovery. Often, this function is associated with a recovery or post-recovery phase of crisis leadership. After the pressure of crisis subsides, post hoc learning can provide important perspectives. However, real-time reflection and assessment may help keep response and recovery on track as well as yield useful insights and lessons.

9. *Improving into the future.* Effective crisis leaders look for ways to use crisis as a stimulus for "a fresh start," as an opportunity for creating a better, more effective organization.[50] Often, the chaos of crisis presents opportunities for innovation.[51] The ideal is for leaders not just to successfully engage and recover from a crisis but to translate the effort into lasting, positive reform that might never have happened otherwise.[52]

10. *Tending to people and to relationships.* Perhaps the most important function of effective crisis leadership, one that cuts across all the other functions and each phase of crisis leadership work, is tending to people and to relationships. Recovery from crisis, no less the survival of an organization, depends on the resilience of its members. And their resilience depends on how leadership understands and responds to the human and social needs, emotions, and behaviors associated with a crisis.[53] Strong, positive social connections can serve as reservoirs of emotional and psychological support that instill confidence and provide means to weather crises well. Indeed, leaders can reduce the duration of a crisis and mitigate its negative effects by addressing the human element before, during, and after a crisis occurs.[54]

We now take a closer look at this last function, focusing specifically on the bright through line of caring.

The Through Line of Caring

In addition to phases and functions, effective crisis leadership is defined by certain qualities.[55] Among them are the readiness, courageousness, resourcefulness, innovativeness, flexibility and adaptability, self-awareness, and resiliency of the leader. Effective crisis leadership is well informed, well organized, innovative, improvisational, and able to tolerate and manage uncertainty and ambiguity. It is also and importantly ethical.

As Paul Argenti explains, effective crisis leadership is "a mixture of head and heart"; it is driven by a "dedication to caring."[56] Indeed it is framed by a mindset concerned with human need.[57] During crisis situations, human need can run wide and deep. The need may be psychological, emotional,

---

[49] James and Wooten (2004).
[50] James and Wooten (2004), Pepper et al. (2010).
[51] Waldron and Wetherbe (2020).
[52] Sharfstein (2018).
[53] Klann (2003), Teo et al. (2017).
[54] Klann (2003).
[55] Anderson (2018), Argenti (2020), Comfort (2007), Dückers (2017), James and Wooten (2004), Pepper et al. (2010), Sharfstein (2018),
[56] Argenti (2020, p. 24, 25).
[57] Flynn (2002).

spiritual, physical, social, material, and financial. It may manifest inside and outside an organization, among organizational members, constituents, and stakeholders. In schools, it is the need, born of crisis, of students, teachers, staff, school leaders, families, and members of surrounding communities.

Philosopher David Bauman argues that crisis leadership is most effective when guided by an ethic of care.[58] An ethic of care emphasizes strengthening relationships and fulfilling responsibilities to others. It emphasizes how one's actions may affect the feelings of others, which is critical for strengthening supportive social relationships to address human need. An ethic of care directs leaders to fulfill the organization's responsibilities to its members and to those outside the organization who depend on it. An ethic of care directs leaders to provide aid and comfort, to address human stress and suffering, and in doing so maintain the social fabric of the organization and strengthen its ability to respond to, recover from, and perhaps become better and stronger from the crisis.

The literature on crisis leadership is replete with references to the importance of caring. Many who have explored crisis leadership in schools give it particular emphasis. Caring is a crucial through line of crisis leadership, relevant to all its functions, orienting them toward preserving and promoting human health, well-being, and success.

Caring School Leadership in Times of Crisis[59]

To understand more fully the role of caring in crisis leadership in schools, we step back to examine the meaning of caring and caring school leadership. We begin by laying out reasons to care about caring in schools in ordinary times and in times of crisis. We examine the meaning of caring and what makes leadership actions and interactions caring. And we present a model of caring school leadership. We apply this model to school leadership during crisis.

Why Care About Caring?

There are four important reasons to care about caring in schools and to work to promote it.

> **Why Care About Caring in Schools?**
>
> 1. Caring is an intrinsic good.
> 2. Caring is crucial to the learning and development of children and youth and their success in school.
> 3. The alternatives to caring are unacceptable.
> 4. Caring is highly variable in schools today.

First, caring is an intrinsic good, elemental of the human condition, and a worthy endeavor in its own right. It is a foundation stone of being moral and a state for which we long and strive. To care for others is to give meaning for our own lives.

---

[58] Bauman (2011).
[59] This section was adapted from Smylie, Murphy, and Louis (2020).

Second, caring is crucial to the learning and development of children and youth and their success in school. It is the bedrock of all successful education. Research repeatedly emphasizes the importance of caring to student engagement, conduct, and academic success. Caring relationships with adults are associated with healthy brain development, cognitive and social-emotional functioning, and the ability to mediate stress, threat, and trauma. Caring is also associated with the development of positive psychological states such as self-concept, self-esteem, self-efficacy, safety, hope, and persistence. It is also associated with children's capacities for prosocial behaviors and resilience, all of which can contribute to academic learning and performance. Moreover, caring can lead to more caring. Children and youth who experience caring from adults and peers are more likely to act in caring ways themselves. Both resilience and replicating caring—paying it forward—may be important as students and schools experience and recover from crisis.

A third reason to care about caring is that the alternatives are unacceptable. Lack of caring or harmful uncaring can impede positive learning and development as well as positive and caring social behavior. Lack of caring can lead to feelings of isolation, antisocial behavior, negative attitudes toward school, and poor academic engagement—all contributing to low academic achievement. Important to our consideration of crisis, lack of caring and support can negatively affect children's ability to regulate stress and manage trauma.

A fourth reason to care about caring in schools is that we cannot assume that caring is present and unproblematic. There is a paradoxical notion that caring is present and strong in schools because caring is what schools are supposed to do. This is an assumption of "spontaneously occurring caring"[60] that is not always born out in student experience. Studies show that substantial portions of students do not see their schools as caring, encouraging places even as educators believe that they are. Moreover, caring is highly variable in schools today, particularly for students of color, students of low socioeconomic backgrounds, low-performing students, and students placed at risk.

Why Care About Caring During Crises?

There are also many reasons why we should care about caring during crises. In addition to the four reasons above, crises can create or intensify human need and amplify the imperative to address them.[61] They can create disruption, damage, and debilitation for students, teachers, staff, and school leaders. They can cause emotional, psychological, and social distress as well as illness, physical harm, and death. Crises can exact financial and property loss, and loss of employment, which may lead to hunger and homelessness. To address these needs—to give care and support and to do so in caring manner—is crucial. As we stated earlier, caring plays an important role in the resilience of children and youth—and adults—in experiencing and recovering from stress and trauma. Inasmuch as the

> **Why Care About Caring in Times of Crisis?**
>
> 1. Crises create new human needs and amplify the need to address them.
> 2. To address the human needs born of crisis is to fulfill a duty of care.
> 3. Even in crisis situations, we cannot assume the presence or emergence of caring.

---

[60] Brechin (1998, p. 2).
[61] Koehn (2020), Sutton (2020).

ability of schools to encounter and recover from crisis is dependent on the health, strength, and resilience of teachers, staff, and leaders, the human need associated with crisis must be addressed.

Research illuminates the types of human need that may arise in schools as they experience crises. In their work on school crisis prevention and intervention, Mary Margaret Kerr and Garry King emphasize that during crisis many children and adults in schools need the "psychological first aid" of emotional support, understanding of their experiences, and a sense of what they might expect going forward.[62] They need information about what they can do in the moment, and they may need psychological and emotional support services, medical care, shelter, and food. In her study of New Zealand schools recovering from earthquakes, Carol Mutch emphasizes the importance to crisis response and recovery of a positive, caring school community and the strong and trusting social relationships that can provide support and care.[63] Likewise, Peter O'Connor and Nozomu Takahashi, in their case studies of principal leadership during large-scale natural disasters, highlight the importance of putting the interests of children before all else, keeping children safe, and providing support and care to address the psychological, emotional, and medical needs of children, staff, and families.[64] Looking across numerous crisis situations, Pepper and his colleagues stress caring for the emotional well-being of students, families, teachers, and staff during any type of crisis.[65] And from a school counseling psychology perspective, Rosemary Thompson points to the importance of assisting people emotionally in recovering from trauma born of crisis.[66]

In addition, we should care about caring during crisis, especially to address the human need born of crisis, to fulfill an affirmative duty of care we assume as educators.[67] This is a duty to do everything reasonably possible to protect students from foreseeable harm, injury, and death. By extension, this is a duty to address those things that if left unaddressed would result in additional harm. It applies to the protection of teachers, staff, and school leaders in the employ of schools and districts. This duty of care is professional, legal, and moral. Philosophers argue that to care, we must assume a responsibility to care. But to assume responsibility is not enough. Joan Tronto contends that a duty of care requires an obligation to care in situations where caring action or reaction is due.[68] Crises certainly are such situations.

Earlier we argued that it is important to care about caring in schools because, in ordinary time, we cannot assume that it is present nor experienced by all. We pointed to the problematic assumption of "spontaneously occurring caring." This tells us that we should care about caring in times of crisis because we cannot assume that caring is present or will emerge when crisis comes. Although it is said that crises can call out our "better angels," it can also be said, in the words attributed to late 19th-century author James Lane Allen, that "adversity does not build character, it reveals it." As organization and management scholar Ian Mitroff and his colleagues observe, many organizations can be insensitive to the social, emotional, psychological, and physical needs of their members in ordinary time and especially when organizations themselves are under the stress of a major crisis.[69] There is no reason to think that this observation does not apply, at least to some degree, to schools.

There is also a strong argument that we should care about caring in schools *before* crises come because caring creates a context, a resource, that helps schools respond to and recover from crisis.

---

[62] Kerr and King (2019, p. 178).
[63] Mutch (2015).
[64] O'Connor and Takahashi (2014).
[65] Pepper et al. (2010).
[66] Thompson (2004)
[67] MacNeil and Topping (2007), Noddings (2013).
[68] Tronto (2005). See also Engster (2005).
[69] Mitroff et al. (1987).

From their analysis of school leadership during different types of crisis situations, Pepper and his colleagues observe that "organizational strength remains the best predictor for whether an organization will successfully surmount a crisis."[70] Successful responses to crisis, they continue, turn on the degree to which schools have previously cultivated trusting, empowering, caring relationships among the principal, teachers, student, parents, and the larger community. Quoting Anna Switzer, principal of an elementary school in New York City in the aftermath of 9/11: "You can only be the school on the day of the crisis that you were the day before the crisis."[71] Mutch makes exactly the same point, emphasizing the importance of an existing culture of care built up over a period of time. When crises came to the schools in her study, the positive relationships and the community of care that principals had cultivated led students and teachers to be and feel cared for and supported. They started caring more, and they started helping others.

What Is Caring?

We use the word "caring" to represent the qualities of relationships and of actions and interactions that exhibit concern, provide support, nurture, meet students' and adults' needs, and promote their success and well-being. Caring is not simply caring about—that is, having concern or sentiment for someone of something. It is important to care about students, teachers, and their success. However, it is another thing to be caring of them. Caring includes but goes beyond feelings of concern and sentiment to actions and inter-actions—practices—of being in relationships with others and achieving particular aims on their behalf. Caring means both worrying and actively doing something about those worries.

> Caring includes but goes beyond feelings of concern and sentiment to actions and interactions—practices—of being in relationships with others and achieving particular aims on their behalf. Caring means both worrying and actively doing something about those worries.

Caring is not defined by specific actions or interactions. Nor is it defined by a particular set of activities that are necessarily different from those in which one regularly engages. Caring is not necessarily another responsibility that adds to one's job description and workload. All actions and interactions—all activities— can be viewed through a lens of caring. Again, caring, as we define it, is a quality of relationships—the matter, manner, and motivation of personal and professional action and interaction.

What Makes Actions and Interactions Caring?

We believe that three elements together make actions and interactions caring: (1) the pursuit of particular aims; (2) the activation of positive virtues and mindsets; and (3) competent enactment. These elements form a system of antecedents to caring. Each may have personal and professional dimensions. Moreover, the expression of these elements in caring action and interaction may be affected positively or negatively by a variety of interrelated contexts—interpersonal, organizational, and extra organizational.

1. *Pursuit of the aims of caring* Caring is neither aimless nor agnostic in purpose. For actions and interactions to be caring, they must focus on achieving particular objectives. Caring aims to promote the functioning, general well-being, and success of others, as individuals and as groups. Caring addresses particular needs of others and promotes their interests. Caring aims

---

[70] Pepper et al. (2010, p. 12).
[71] Pepper et al. (2010, p. 12).

to help others grow and flourish in their own right. Caring is something framed as a response to pain, suffering, and trouble. But it can be proactive and an affirmative expression of joy and celebration. Caring can also be a worthwhile endeavor in itself.

Caring can aim to address particular needs, problems, and concerns. It can seek to provide tangible benefits, the manner in which and the motivation by which they are provided being as important as the benefits themselves. These benefits can come from particular services and provisions. Caring can aim to promote certain benefits—social, psychological, emotional, and behavioral—that accrue from being in caring relationships and feeling cared for. Finally, caring can aim to promote further caring.

It is not difficult to think about particular aims of education that relate to caring. We consider the general purposes of schooling to provide for students' safety and nurturance; support their learning, development, independence, self-reliance, prosocial relationships, and ability to function in and contribute to community; promote academic success and general well-being; and prepare students for work, further educational pursuits, and citizenship. It is also not difficult to think about the aims of caring leadership in relation to crisis, as we discussed earlier.

2. *Activation of positive virtues and mindsets* A second element of caring consists of positive virtues and mindsets that are brought to the pursuit of the aims of caring. These virtues include compassion, empathy, patience, sympathy, and kindness. They include fairness and justice, authenticity, humility, and vulnerability. They also include prudence, transparency, honesty, trustworthiness, and respect for others and their integrity.

Three positive mindsets are particularly important to caring in ordinary times and in times of crisis. The first is attentiveness to others. If caring is to address others' needs and interests, one must be attentive to understand, deeply and genuinely, who persons are and what their needs, concerns, interests, and situations might be.

Another mindset is motivational orientation. If caring truly means acting on behalf of others, one must be motivated accordingly, and this orientation cannot be diminished by attention to one's own needs and self-interests. Attentiveness and motivational orientation toward others do not lead to permissiveness or abdication of responsibility. Rather they become a positive basis for the fulfillment of personal and professional responsibility.

A third mindset consists of personal and professional identities related to caring. How persons see themselves as caring or uncaring human beings and as capable or incapable of caring will likely affect their efforts to be caring. Likewise, how persons see themselves in a professional role, what they perceive the norms of the profession to require of them, and what they perceive as others' expectations for them in their role may influence caring.

3. *Competent enactment* In addition to aims and positive virtues and mindsets, to be caring requires competency. Effort and sincerity are important and may be appreciated, but particular actions and interactions may not be perceived as caring or helpful if they are uninformed, inadequate, misguided, or poorly performed.

In caring, one important area of competency is knowledge and authentic understanding of others and their needs, problems, joys, concerns, and situations. If educators have inaccurate understanding of who students are and what they want and need, they may make well-meaning attempts to be caring but ultimately miss the mark as to what is caring and helpful in the eyes of students. The same applies to teachers and staff. Developing such understanding is related to one's ability to inquire, listen and hear, observe and see, assess and understand, and learn about others. Social-emotional intelligence is particularly important to caring and caring school leadership. Also important is understanding persons' and groups' races, classes, genders, sexual orientations, languages, culture, religious beliefs, and relevant contexts.

A second area of competency concerns understanding the relative effectiveness of strategies to address the needs and concerns of others and to promote their interests. This includes knowledge and skills to engage these strategies successfully. Caring requires knowledge and skill to develop or select, adapt, and enact practices that pursue the aims of caring; that bring virtues of caring to life; and that align with understanding others, their situations, and their joys, needs, and concerns. Caring further requires the ability to wrestle with ethical and practical dilemmas posed by different and competing needs and considerations.

A third area of competency concerns knowledge of self and the ability to develop and deepen one's own capacity for caring. Knowledge of self involves understanding one's orientations and inclinations, strengths and limitations, and predispositions and prejudices. Recognizing the sources of one's fears and joys may be crucial in thinking and acting in a caring manner in ordinary time and in times of crisis.

A fourth area of competency, especially important to school leaders, consists of knowledge and skills for developing caring among others and creating organizational contexts conducive to caring. This includes understanding how to think about caring as a property of classroom and school organization, not only as a quality of interpersonal relationships. It includes knowledge and skill related to professional learning and development and organizational change. It encompasses knowledge and skill to create supportive structures and processes, to design work and social arrangements, and to develop organizational cultures imbued with the virtues and mindsets of caring.

A Model of Caring School Leadership

Following from this discussion, we define caring school leadership as leadership that is itself caring, which proceeds from the aims of caring, positive virtues and mindsets related to caring, and competencies for the expression of caring in action and interaction. We believe that caring is not a special domain of leadership, nor is it a discrete set of leadership strategies. Although its practice may vary depending on the people involved, interpersonal and organizational contexts, and the environments surrounding the school, it is a quality or property of leadership generally. It is the matter, manner, and motivation of school leadership.

As a quality of relationship, action, and interaction, caring can permeate almost everything that a school leader says and does. It can span all of school leadership work. Any aspect of leadership can be caring, noncaring, or even uncaring. What matters is that a school leader brings the aims, virtues, and mindsets of caring to life through competent action and interaction. The relational aspects of leadership—the trusting interpersonal relationships that leaders form with students, teachers, staff, and parents—lie at the heart of caring school leadership. Yet caring leadership is not confined there. Caring can be infused in developing and promoting a school's mission, vision, and core values. It can be integrated into expectations for teaching and student learning. Caring can be a driving force of academic program development and implementation, of instructional leadership, of providing services for groups of students, and of allocating resources to support teaching and learning. Caring can shape the nature of academic demand and support, testing and accountability, student discipline, and administrative decision-making. Caring can guide programs of outreach to families and the school's community. And, as we will discuss shortly, it can guide school leadership in times of crisis.

These points are captured in our model of caring school leadership in Figure 1.1. This model contains three major components: (1) foundational elements for caring leadership; (2) arenas of caring school leadership practice; and (3) outcomes of caring leadership. Our model traces with arrows relationships among these components and how each relates to others. It does not focus on every aspect of school leadership or how the totality of school leadership work might be performed in a caring manner. Our model is presented with students in mind, but it applies to caring for teachers, staff, parents, and others. Indeed, caring school leadership has as its focus the betterment, well-being, and success of all in the school. Moreover, if caring leadership is to foster systems of caring for students within schools, it must attend to the caring of teachers and staff. It is much more likely for teachers

Figure 1.1

Model of Caring School Leadership

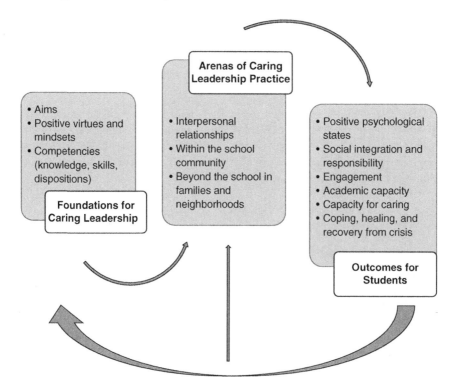

to be caring and supportive of their students if teachers believe they are cared for and supported by school leadership.

Our model shows caring school leadership proceeding from the aims, positive virtues and mindsets, and competencies of caring. It suggests that the presence and strength of these elements enable and shape the character and impact of caring leadership practice. At the center of the model lie three arenas of practices. The first arena where caring leadership is practiced is in interpersonal relationships with students, teachers and staff, parents, and other stakeholders. The second arena is the school community. The third arena for the practice of caring school leadership lies outside the school in families, neighborhoods, and broader environments. These arenas are contexts in which caring leadership is enacted and can be the subjects of caring leadership. For example, caring leadership often is practiced in the context of interpersonal relationships. At the same time, the caring actions and interactions of school leadership may be directed at making interpersonal relationships more caring. Likewise, caring leadership may be enacted in the context of the school organization. At the same time, it might be directed at cultivating the school as a caring community to develop the caring capacity of others and shape organizational conditions to be more supportive of caring.

In the lived work of school leaders, these arenas of practice are often intertwined, but our model does not presume that they are. Our model also allows for the possibility of one arena of caring school leadership practice compensating for another.

We expect principals to act in caring ways and provide caring support to students with whom they are able to form trusting interpersonal relationships. At the same time, to ensure that every student receives caring support, principals can promote teacher and staff caring so that each student experiences caring relationships with a number of adults in the school. By doing this, principals need not take on all the work themselves. Principals will be much more effective if they develop the capacity of others, work in partnership with others, and guide and support others to step up and be better at caring.

The right side of the model shows student outcomes that we expect from caring school leadership. The model identifies several types of outcomes important to students that we discussed earlier—positive psychological states, social integration and responsibility, and the capacity for achieving goals, engagement, academic success, and capacity for caring. To these outcomes we can add the outcomes of coping, healing, and recovery from crisis. The model indicates that the stronger the practices of caring school leadership in different arenas of practice, the more likely caring's benefits will accrue. Students benefit most when the totality of caring they experience is strong and positive. The model does not depict outcomes of caring leadership that we might expect for teachers, staff, and others. However, we expect that the types of outcomes would be similar. In times of crisis, we believe that caring leadership would contribute to coping, healing, and recovery among adults as well as students.

The major parts of the model are laid out in linear order, indicating with one-way arrows that the foundational elements of caring shape caring leadership practice and, in turn, promote the outcomes of caring. The model indicates with feedback arrows that outcomes can shape the nature of caring leadership practice and the three foundational elements of caring. For example, students' responses to positive experiences of caring may motivate leaders to continue those practices. When students ignore or resist particular actions or interactions intended to be caring, attentive leaders may seek more information, reflect, and perhaps alter what they are doing. Although it does not depict them, our model recognizes the importance of dynamic and interrelated interpersonal, organizational, and extra organizational contexts. Although the arrows in the model suggest a sequential order of elements, the reality of leadership generally and caring school leadership in particular is more nonlinear and dynamic.

Examples of Practice

We have stated that caring is not a special domain of school leadership, nor is it a discrete set of leadership strategies. It can permeate everything a school leader says and does. Caring is the matter, manner, and motivation of the whole of school leadership, a quality of its enactment. The practice of caring school leadership is situational and it is dynamic.

And so it is with the practice of caring school leadership during times of crisis. We can imagine how the work, the functions of crisis leadership, can be practiced in caring ways. The work of crisis prevention and preparation; of response, containment, and damage control; and of recovery can be seen and pursued through the lens of caring. Reinforcing the school's mission and core values and setting priorities for the future can bring to the fore the aims and virtues of caring, as can promoting meaning and sensemaking about crisis and how to engage and recover from it. Communications can promote the aims and virtues of caring and be executed in a manner that anticipates and addresses the needs and concerns of those affected by crisis. Acquiring and allocating resources can be guided similarly. The work of learning from crisis can focus on the role of caring, and the work of improving into the future can place caring at the top of the agenda. Certainly, caring can and should be at the heart of tending to people and relationships.

Practices that we consider examples of caring school leadership can be found in several studies of schools in crisis situations. In her review of responses to different crises including Hurricane Katrina, Mutch describes how principals helped children process events without dwelling too much on the aspects they find distressing, and how they helped students talk to caring and trusted adults, find support from their peers, and express their feelings through creative activities.[72] She describes how principals tried to reintroduce stability by returning to normal routines or by adopting new ones. These principals spoke frequently to students and teachers about school values, especially love, support and empathy, hospitality, and care. They made special effort to check in regularly with all members of their school communities to see how everyone was faring, learn about their needs, and assess how the school might be able to help. They kept their eyes and ears open for indicators of need. These principals drew on the trust and the social-emotional support of relationships cultivated before the crisis. Above and across all, they put others' interests above their own.

In O'Connor and Takahashi's case studies of New Zealand and Japanese schools recovering from earthquakes, we see principals putting the interests of children before all else, keeping them safe, attending to their needs, and managing their anxiety.[73] They also prioritized the needs of staff and families. These leaders took control with an air of calm and kindness. Practical needs were addressed—medical attention, shelter, water, and sanitation facilities were secured. While power was out, they found new ways to access information and employed multiple means to communicate with parents. These school leaders used community resources to give extra support to children and their families and, in the process, strengthened school–community relationships forged from common experience. When it was time to return to school, these school leaders and their teachers planned how they would welcome back students, provide safe opportunities for them to make sense of their experiences, and help address students' ongoing fear and anxiety.

Other examples of caring leadership practices can be found in works from the field of school counseling and psychology.[74]

To help you in your own practice of leading schools during times of crisis, we present a guide to help you engage the stories to come.

---

[72] Mutch (2015).
[73] O'Connor and Takahashi (2014).
[74] For example, Kerr and King (2019), Thompson (2004).

Guide for Engaging the Stories

This guide begins with an overview of caring school leadership practices that are illustrated in the stories. It concludes with two sets of questions for reflecting upon and discussing the stories. The first set aims to promote deeper understanding of different aspects of caring and caring leadership during crisis. The second is designed to help you apply insights and lessons from the stories to your own situation and practice.

Overview of Practices

The stories in this book took place in two arenas for the practice of caring school leadership. The first are interpersonal relationships of school leaders with students, teachers, and staff. The second is the community inside the school. Regardless of the arena of practice, each story makes visible in one way or another the aims, positive virtues and mindsets, and competencies of caring. Many illustrate the outcomes of caring to students, teachers, and staff. As we mentioned earlier, not all of our stories are clearly positive. You may find some troublesome, and some reveal problems that may arise out of the best intentions.

Many aspects of caring school leadership practice are illustrated in these stories. We do not pretend that they capture the full range and situational variations of this practice. Some of the most important aspects of practice in these stories are listed below. Look for and reflect upon them as you read. Stay attuned to other aspects of caring leadership practice you may see.[75]

Aspects of a Caring School Leadership Practice

1. *Being present.* It is difficult to imagine being able to know students and staff, understand their needs and interests, and be caring of them if school leaders are not present and accessible. Presence is physical (and virtual) and mental, the latter meaning that school leaders must be continually mindful of others to be caring of them. Look for different ways that school leaders are present in these stories.

2. *Attending and inquiring.* Several stories illustrate different ways that school leaders can be attentive to students and teachers to know and understand them, their needs, and concerns, so as to be caring of them, and ways that school leaders can be similarly attentive to school community. Look for ways that school leaders may observe, inquire, hear, and listen. Look for ways that school leaders may try to see crisis through the eyes of others, especially students.

3. *Expressing empathy, compassion, kindness, and altruism.* Look for the enactment of these and other positive virtues and mindsets of caring described in the introduction.

4. *Acting on behalf of others.* These stories show examples of different ways in which school leaders act or give care on behalf of students and teachers to help and support them during crisis. This assistance includes emotional, psychological, medical, and material support. Several stories show how acting on behalf of students and teachers can conflict with district rules and how school leaders bend these rules toward students and teachers rather than bend students and teachers toward the rules.

---

[75] An in-depth discussion of these and other caring leadership practices can be found in *Caring School Leadership*, and additional stories of these and other aspects of practice can be found in *Stories of Caring School Leadership*.

5. *Promoting the core values and purposes of the school.* Several stories illustrate how school leaders stay focused and help others stay focused during crisis on the core values and purposes that define the school community. Among these values, especially in times of crisis, is putting the health, safety, and well-being of students, teachers, staff, and families at the fore. These values include mutual commitment to and responsibility for the care of others. Look for ways that school leaders emphasize and enforce values of caring and support, respect, honor, love, empathy, compassion, and importantly optimism and hope.

6. *Creating means of social connection.* In these stories are illustrations of ways that school leaders provide opportunities for social connection. Even as crises separate people physically and emotionally, school leaders can keep interpersonal connections strong, checking in with everyone, building links, and creating occasions for togetherness to work or to maintain social and emotional attachment.

7. *Making meaning.* Several stories highlight being aware of things that give people meaning at school and in their work. They provide examples of school leaders helping students, teachers, staff, and parents make meaning of crises and the implications for themselves, their families, and their schools. We see school leaders find ways to maintain traditions and routines and preserve symbols large and small that help bind the school community together. Several stories reveal the importance of history to school community, even as a new chapter in that history is being written.

8. *Communicating.* Several stories focus on the importance of communication—formal and informal, individual and corporate—as a means of being in community during crises. These stories illustrate the importance of clarity, authenticity, truthfulness, accuracy, transparency, currentness, and positivity. They illustrate the importance of keeping the school community informed of the crisis, being real while maintaining optimism.

9. *Securing resources and removing obstacles.* A number of stories show leaders actively seeking and acquiring resources to help their schools encounter and recover from crisis. These include financial and material resources as well as therapeutic resources, such as professional support and counselors. Several stories show leaders connecting members of their school communities to sources of support beyond the school. There are examples of school leaders creating safe spaces for emotional expression and repair. We also see leaders unleash the resources of strong, positive social relationships once a crisis occurs. Some stories tell of leaders working to remove structural and other obstacles to caring and support.

10. *Accepting responsibility for and sharing leadership.* These stories illustrate the many ways in which school leaders directly assume responsibility for leading during crisis. Look for examples where school leaders also bring others into this leadership, creating opportunities for student and teacher "voice" and influence and in the process improving the effectiveness of crisis leadership and strengthening the school community.

The stories reveal several important qualities of caring leadership such as vulnerability, humility, and a willingness of leaders to do what they ask others to do. They include creativity and, importantly in crisis situations, bricoleurship—creatively constructing something out of a range of available things. Several stories show the importance of being able to make tough calls. Many others show the importance of protecting the safety and integrity of the school community and its members, even as such actions pose risk to the school leader. Last but not least, these stories show the importance of leadership that is both present in the midst of a crisis as well as looking to a better future when the crisis subsides.

As you read, reflect upon, and discuss these stories, consider the following questions.

Questions That Promote Understanding

1. How does each story reflect the three foundational elements of caring school leadership described in the introduction: (a) the aims of caring, (b) positive virtues and mindsets of caring, and (c) competent enactment? In what ways might these three elements be strong or weak in the story? How might these strengths or weaknesses shape the actions and interactions of the school leader and any outcomes apparent? How might caring in the story be seen as everyday work, even during crisis, rather than as something extra that school leaders do? How can caring demonstrated by school leaders help others to be more caring?

2. How might the school leader's assumptions, understandings, and biases affect the way each story unfolds and the subsequent outcomes?

3. How might different contexts affect the story?
   - The nature of different types of crisis situations
   - The qualities and characteristics of interpersonal relationships
   - The organizational context of the school or setting and the surrounding environment

4. What professional and personal ethical issues do these stories raise? What legal issues? Where such issues are apparent, what advice would you give the school leader to address them?

5. In what ways are understanding of students, teachers, and staff as persons, learners, and employees important to the actions and interactions of school leaders? In what ways do school leaders' efforts to further such knowledge and understanding contribute to their ability to be caring? In what ways do insufficient or incorrect knowledge and understanding make caring more difficult or less effective?

6. How do these stories help you better understand the types of assistance that might be helpful to students, teachers, staff, and others? How do these stories help you better understand how the way such assistance is given may affect the outcome?

7. In these stories, how might school leader caring contribute to the ability and the motivation of others to be more caring of each other? How might the context of crisis help promote or impede caring among others?

8. What do you see as the main lesson or lessons of each story? If you were to write a moral for each story, what would it be?

9. What is your personal reaction to each story? Why are you reacting this way? What might be influencing your thinking?

10. Imagine that the school leader in the story asked you, "What do you think about what I said and what I did?" Looking through the eyes of the different people in the story, how would you respond? What advice would you give to this school leader?

Questions That Prompt Application

1. How might your own assumptions, preconceptions, and points of view influence how you read and make meaning of these stories? Jot down a few of your assumptions and preconceptions. Does the exercise of jotting them down prompt you to any action? If so, what would it be?

2. Consider your understanding of yourself as a caring person and a caring educator and leader, including your strengths and weaknesses in being caring of others. Consider your understanding of what the professional role of a school leader requires of you; what your situation calls on you to do; and what your students, your teachers and staff, and your school's parents and community expect of you. How does your thinking and sense of self affect how you practice caring generally and in times of crisis? Think of a moment of crisis that happened during the past 12 months and jot down how your sense of self affected how you practiced caring in that situation.

3. Put yourself in the position of the school leader who is the focus of each story. Would you think and act in the same way in the situation described? Why or why not? In what ways might you think and act differently? Why? Select a story that parallels something that has happened in your leadership practice. How did you behave in that situation? What are the similarities and differences between how you practiced caring and how the school leaders in the story practiced caring?

4. For each story, recall a similar, actual situation in your school. How would you retell the story for your own setting, with yourself as the focal school leader? In what ways is your story similar? In what ways is your story different? To what do you attribute these similarities and differences?

5. After reading the stories, which caring practices or leadership strategies would you like to incorporate into your own leadership practice? Why? Which practices would you not want to emulate? Why?

The Stories

1. Through the Eyes of Children

Told by the executive director of an early childhood community organization

Much of the community dialogue around protecting our children from COVID-19 has focused on the masks, gloves, and disinfectant wipes that are used to minimize our exposure to this virus. These are important measures, but perhaps there is more than protection. Maybe the imperative is not the urgent call for disinfection but the more subtle, silent call that is less about protection and more about understanding.

Even if children aren't speaking, we know that they are listening, watching, and experiencing an event with us. With fewer coping resources than adults, they work to make sense of the world around them.

Infants won't understand what COVID-19 is, but they will react to adult emotions and the feelings of insecurity that arise when routines are disrupted and caregivers show signs of anxiety. Similarly, a 3-year-old might not understand CDC reports describing the coronavirus but will be acutely aware of additional tension in the house, the fear that adults are feeling, and the unusual occurrence of schools being ordered closed by the government. Whether children cope successfully might depend upon our ability to understand what they see and feel, acknowledge their emotional needs, be in touch with our own emotions, and bring them into our dialogues. Let's integrate children into our journey through this pandemic. Let's see them as important partners who need reassurance, help coping, and a solid understanding of what is happening around them. Let's see them as partners through whose eyes we can see how to be caring. That is our path forward.

Our children see and try to make sense of the world around them. It can be a frightening or comforting place. They can see a world full of despair and tragedy. But they can also see a world full of the strength and compassion of those around us.

On the television news a building ignites, trapping a mother and her two children on the top floor. What seems like the end of a tragic story takes a turn when firefighters, defying their own sense of fear, find the family hiding in a back room of the burning building and deliver them to safety. An elderly woman has a heart attack and feels sure that she will spend the last moments of her life alone on her kitchen floor, only to be seen by a postal worker who, delivering mail, noticed that something was amiss. Later, the letter carrier, squinting into the light of the cameras, said, "Anyone would have done what I did." An interviewer speaks with a retired nurse, who, seeing that there was a need for more hospital personnel, stepped out of retirement and offered to serve at a local hospital that was overwhelmed with its efforts to combat the COVID-19 pandemic. When asked why, the nurse said that times like this called for extraordinary sacrifice. The nurse added that people had to work together if they wanted to improve the human condition.

There are common threads in all of these stories. Compassion. Kindness. Sacrifice. While we are confronted with the risks and frailties of the human experience, we are reminded that we can rely upon the worst of times to cultivate the best in people. When the community faces a crisis, the helpers, heroes, and great people emerge. They shine, and if we look, we can see them. Our children can see them too.

I'm reminded of a magical quote by Fred Rogers. In a public service announcement recorded to comfort and assure children after the tragedy of 9/11, he said, "When I was a boy, and I would see scary things in the news, my mother would say to me, 'Look for the helpers. You will always find people who are helping.' And I've found that's true. In fact, it's one of the best things about our wonderful world."

When our children see scary things around them, we can tell them to look for the helpers. When children in nursery schools and day-care centers are under stress or experience trauma in their lives, we can tell them to look for the helpers. I ask their teachers, their schools' directors, and their caregivers to remind themselves of what they were like as children and to be helpers. Let our children know that if they look around, they will find the helpers because we are there for them—the teachers, directors, leaders, childcare givers, doctors, nurses, technicians, specialists, and clinicians leading the fight for our community's well-being!

While we remain in our homes during the pandemic, and even as we venture out again and back to school, an army of kind humans march off to work to fight on the front line and preserve the future for all of us. Let us be the helpers our children will look for and find. The best response to fear might be hope. Add gratitude, and darkness doesn't stand a chance.

You Are Not Alone—Zara Campos, Grade 5

2. Speak Life

Told by the principal of an urban public elementary school

I do this work from a place of love *and* a place of pain. An educator of color who started her journey in education as a little Black girl at a Title 1 inner-city school, I was too often underestimated, second-guessed, confronted by racism, and surrounded by lowered expectations. I fought hard to prove myself time and time again to transform trials and tribulations into triumph. But my degrees, awards, and accolades mean nothing if people don't know my "why." The reason I am in this work is because I care . . . so deeply, in fact, that it hurts sometimes. My experiences shaped me into the school leader I have become today and deepened my commitment to this work.

When the COVID-19 pandemic hit, and the world quickly pivoted to remote learning, forcing school leaders to redesign the entire educational system overnight, teachers were hailed as heroes—that is, until people grew weary of quarantining. Protests to reopen schools denigrated virtual learning, negating the time, energy, resources, and planning poured into this model. Health experts and politicians pressured schools to reopen before securing adequate funding or further discussion of the extensive resources needed to make in-person learning safe for all. Teachers were faulted for fear and anxiety over COVID, accused of not wanting to teach. Administrators were blamed for COVID outbreaks and disjointed educational experiences caused by school closures and pivots back and forth between virtual and in-person learning. Educators were forced to choose between their lives and livelihoods. Initially hailed as heroes, they were now being told to teach or quit.

And then there were principals like me caught between a rock and a hard place. Rarely acknowledged in the trenches, we were invisible, working tirelessly behind the scenes to create safe, positive learning environments under a barrage of complaints and criticisms. Few seemed to understand the complexities of our role and the endless amount of work it entailed. We were torn. On the one hand, we were aware of the disproportionate impact of the pandemic on communities of color and individuals with disabilities, and we owned the importance of remote learning. On the other hand, we recognized a dire need for students who were unsuccessful learning online to return to a brick-and-mortar building for in-person instruction. Principals were also caught in the political crosshairs of school boards, teachers' unions, government officials, health experts, employees, and families who

all had competing interests, needs, and motivations. There was a national assumption that learning in person was best, but at what cost? Closer examinations of historical achievement and opportunity gaps between demographic groups called this into question, but who would be courageous enough to challenge this assumption? This was a prime opportunity to reimagine education by revolutionizing virtual learning, but were we missing the moment in this push to return to the status quo? Moreover, we were battling not just one pandemic but two—the pandemic of racial injustice evidenced by rampant examples of police brutality captured on video.

So, I set about preparing for a year like no other. I updated my will and life insurance policy and got my financial affairs in order. I couldn't care for my family or my school community without first taking care of myself. Like on an airplane, I had to place the metaphorical oxygen mask on myself before putting it on those who rely on me. Educators were being ordered to march to the front lines of a war that we hadn't signed up for. Yet, we pressed onward.

As a kid, I was taught to hold my head up high with an omnipresent smile. Never let 'em see you sweat. Don't put your business out in the street. And Never. Ever. Cry. I learned early on that the feelings of little Black girls like me weren't held in as high regard as my peers. I didn't have the privilege of showing emotions without being seen as a threat, weak, or portrayed as a mad Black woman. These life lessons followed me into school leadership.

I learned to model calmness and composure in the midst of raging storms as the world burned around me. And in 2020, it literally burned. From wildfires to fiery protests against racial injustice, flames lit the night sky, etching embers into our hearts and searing them into our minds. In the wake of the George Floyd protests spanning from coast to coast, I fought flashbacks of Walter Scott, the unarmed Black man shot in the back by police in Charleston, South Caroling, on April 4, 2015. I knew him well. To me, he was far more than a statistic. A former deacon at my church, "Deacon Scott" was a lead singer in our gospel choir, dynamic drummer, and my former mentor in the music ministry. I stifled tears reflecting upon memories of The Emmanuel 9, murdered in cold blood just over the bridge downtown during Bible study by a self-proclaimed white nationalist itching to start a race war. I relived the dichotomy of despair and hope during President Barack Obama's soul-stirring rendition of "Amazing Grace" as I sat in the pews at Reverend Clementa Pinckney's funeral. Rage swelled within me when Black churches, including mine, were vandalized by gunshots in the aftermath of these events in my hometown. I remembered fearing for my personal safety and that of my children, who were afraid to attend church after these incidents. But I couldn't share these emotions out loud. Sharing emotions isn't safe for people who look like me.

The crises of 2020—social justice, public health, and the ensuing economic crisis—brought the fight to my front door once again as loved ones became infected with COVID and died. Then, members of my school community contracted COVID. With so many casualties of the pandemic, I felt helpless. People looked to me for guidance, leadership, counsel, and answers. But how could I help them when I was waging the same war and fighting the same battles?

Speak life.

The answer came to me swiftly and clearly. My life's purpose was hiding in plain sight within the meaning of my name—"life" in Swahili. After the murders of Breonna Taylor, George Floyd, and Ahmaud Arbery, I could remain stoic no longer. I defied past messages not to emote, embracing moments of vulnerability with my staff during Zoom meetings and in weekly email updates. I shared my personal stories of overcoming racial trauma, empowering others to do the same. Allies felt inspired to take action. When educators asked me, "What can we do?" I seized the opportunity to enlist their assistance to disrupt dysfunctional cycles in our schools. I interrogated inequitable policies and practices in education, acknowledging the legacy arm of Jim Crow deeply embedded within the American educational system through the school-to-prison pipeline, overidentification of Black Indigenous and People of Color (BIPOC) students into special education and disciplinary systems. Collaboratively with school teams, I set about actively dismantling those systems at my own school through anti-racism and culturally responsive teaching. We began shifting the calculus from a culture of blame and shame to an oasis of opportunity and hope. We celebrated students' accomplishments and recognized them as children of promise rather than children with problems. I charged my school community to . . .

Speak life.

During the 2020 presidential election, I organized support groups for staff to provide safe spaces for adults to share feelings. I modeled vulnerability to encourage them to provide similar safe spaces for their students. As I transitioned from one school community to another during the pandemic, I encountered new challenges of connecting with people I had never met before in person, people I wouldn't get to meet in person for many months. New challenges . . . how would I build trust, provide social and emotional support, and keep it all together? Lead by listening.

Speak life.

I encouraged educators experiencing emotional exhaustion. Compassion fatigue. Burnout. I pressed forward, observing classrooms in person, donning personal protective equipment—my mask, face shield, gloves—and heading into the thick of things to show teachers that I would never ask them to do something that I was not willing to do myself. This was warfare against an invisible enemy, and I would not abandon my troops on the front lines. I offered words of praise and dropped positive notes and messages in their mailboxes, inboxes, and virtual meeting chat boxes. I chose to . . .

Speak life.

But this mantra proved especially difficult when my dad, who lived several states away, was rushed to the hospital at the launch of in-person learning. Although his illness wasn't COVID-related, it was life-threatening. I couldn't visit him due to travel restrictions and hospital guidelines. In the midst of this, I was in the process of hiring for several open teaching positions while fielding anxious COVID questions, concerns, and angst from staff and families. The next month, I lost two close members of our church family within a week of each other. One was like my adopted grandmother. My mother, who was their pastor, eulogized them both while serving as the primary caregiver of my ailing father. I admired her strength, in awe of her drive to keep moving forward despite her circumstances. I attended the virtual funeral services and moments later logged on to a mandatory Zoom call with my superintendent. The expectation to function normally under circumstances that were anything but took a toll. But there was no time to stop, breathe, exhale, or grieve. I held out hope for the holidays, but the seasons came and went with only virtual visits on Zoom, Amazon Echo, and FaceTime because I didn't want to potentially expose anyone to the virus. When my staff shared their own stories of spending their first holidays isolated away from loved ones, I empathized deeply. As hard as it was, with a heavy heart and tears stinging my eyes, I realized now more than ever that I desperately needed to . . .

Speak life.

Then, my husband was furloughed just before the Thanksgiving and Christmas holidays, his organization being the latest COVID-19 casualty in our lives. We didn't know how we were going to make ends meet to support our four school-age children but held onto hope that this season wouldn't last always. In the face of adversity, I chose to rise. Phone calls punctuated my mornings, evenings, weekends, and holidays with the unfortunate news that another person I knew had tested positive for COVID. As I listened empathically to heartfelt stories from families who had lost as many as six relatives during the course of the pandemic while still being expected to work and send their kids to school, my heart ached. Why couldn't the world stop spinning for a minute? Why were so many people intent on plowing full steam ahead without acknowledging the impact of prolonged crisis management? The needs were so great, and they were all laid at my feet to fix, respond, answer . . . to save. But how could I save them when I couldn't even save myself? Were my words making a difference? Yet, I heard the resounding moral imperative.

Speak life.

I couldn't fix it all. Silver and gold had I none, but such as I had, I was willing to give. Words of Life. Hope. Truth. Inspiration. And so I shared them freely and unapologetically, realizing there was a great deal of uncertainty in the air, bringing with it anxiety, fear, anger, disillusionment, and questioning. I found that these questions often led to blame. Why weren't teachers doing more? Why wasn't the principal doing more? Why weren't school districts doing more? And then came rationalizations and swerving outside of our lanes.

Although these reactions were understandable, this type of communication was not helpful. I solicited the patience and understanding of my school community while sorting out the messy nuances in this COVID era. No one had all the answers, not even the experts. This was new territory for all of us. The coronavirus itself was novel, although the pandemic of racism had a long, ugly history imbuing the fabric of the American conscience. If there was any silver lining, it would be that there was finally an acknowledgment and renewed energy to fix what was broken. Federal, state, district, and school-level policies were being reviewed and rewritten for these changing times. New challenges in this new school year offered new perspectives and new opportunities to shift our thinking and embrace a growth mindset. I implored my team to lean into discomfort. We now had the opportunity to live out the true meaning of our mission. It wouldn't be easy, but we could do it as long as we supported each other through it all. We were compelled to . . .

Speak life.

I acknowledged the real impact of COVID on our school community. For affected members, there were feelings of isolation, loneliness, sadness, anger, fear, guilt, and shame. We were all dealing with loss and grief on some level. In moments of uncertainty when there were more questions than answers, I challenged our community to uphold each other and treat each other with grace and love. Speak kindly to each other. Watch our tone of voice. Ask politely rather than demand. Don't complain. Offer solutions. Work collaboratively. Assume best intentions. Agree to disagree. Don't sweat the small stuff. Avoid negative communication patterns and intentionally hunt the good stuff. The task ahead?

Speak life.

Things began to change, not necessarily for the better or worse but . . . different . . . perhaps more meaningfully. People began to truly see each other and sit with each other in our discomfort to offer consolation. They shared personal stories of impact. The impact has been felt far and wide by students and families struggling to make sense of it all. But in the midst of the darkness, a glimmer of hope, a sliver of sunlight . . . and then a glorious daybreak.

Speak life.

There is so much more to leadership than meets the eye. Like an iceberg, only 10 percent is visible above the surface, but the greatest mass lies beneath the waves. We have to trust each other, respect each other, and honor each other's humanity with dignity and humility. Leadership without love is nothing more than empty words, a "sounding brass and a tinkling cymbal" (1 Cor. 13:13). Our words have power. To lead with love, we must be willing to . . .

Speak. Life.

3. Giving Ourselves Permission to Be Human

Told by the principal of an urban public high school

When our governor issued the COVID Stay Home order and schools were closed in March 2020, it was a whirlwind to figure out how to move to distance learning. Our district was not one to one with computers at the time. It was a heavy lift to get technology to all the kids and help teachers learn the online tools they needed to teach. Everyone was highly stressed.

I know intellectually that modeling vulnerability is important when leading for change, but it doesn't come naturally to me. I was conscious of allowing myself to show feelings and affirm feelings with my staff. One day, in an online staff meeting with 140 attendees, I addressed the issue of stress head-on. I said we have to give ourselves permission to be human with each

other and give grace to our colleagues and our students. We also have to expect it to be difficult.

I shared with everyone that earlier in the week, during an online meeting of all the high school principals, I had turned off my camera and walked away in tears. My staff knows that's not my norm! Saying that out loud was not easy, but I heard back from teachers that it gave them permission to feel however they were feeling and know it was OK. We continued to honor emotion and found that naming it was a good way to move through it.

We began the 2020–2021 school year remotely. At the end of the first day, I had an online check-in meeting with staff. We agreed that it was hard not to be together in person. Teachers were glad that student attendance had been high. But it had been rough to be separated physically and have to teach online.

I shared with them that I had cried in the car on the way to school that morning, driving to an empty building. A teacher shared that she had cried over lunch. We all agreed that school was happening and we were grateful for the technology to teach remotely. But it was still hard. And it was OK that we felt that way.

Hold My Hand—Grace Deal, Grade 9

4. Building a Family

Told by a director at a suburban K–12 independent school

Watching the determination in Margaret's face and hearing the resoluteness in her voice gave me hope and confidence in our decision to have on-campus learning during the time of COVID. "Lower School students learn best on campus" and "Remote learning does not work for our youngest learners," and "We can do this safely within our Lower School bubble," Margaret would share during our summer senior leadership team meetings. Lifting and leading during a crisis, like the time of COVID, takes an enormous amount of strength, skill, and stamina, all qualities Margaret possesses.

I have always admired Margaret, an exceptional school leader who leads with her heart and encourages all in her sphere of influence to be the best human beings they can be—students, teachers, and parents. Starting every Lower School staff meeting building community whether it takes 5 or 15 minutes using a sharing out strategy, *News or No News*, Margaret has created a faculty family whose members care deeply for one another and in turn care deeply for the students in their charge. Authentic, compassionate, positive, supportive, and humble—Margaret leads the Lower School, a small but mighty division of our larger school.

We welcomed a new head of school in July 2020. Upon arriving, he shared two goals for the upcoming school year with our senior leadership team: (1) maintain the health and safety of the school community and (2) provide an excellent on-campus education for our students. We were one of the few schools in our area—independent, parochial, or public—that opened for in-person hybrid learning in Fall 2020. Local health authorities, the general public, and our own teachers were skeptical of our decision to welcome students to campus.

As a member of the senior leadership team, I had also mixed feelings about the decision.

What would it be like to have students on campus? Would it be safe for the students? Safe for the adults? Convinced that Lower School students needed to be educated on campus and confident that adults and students could adhere to health and safety protocols put in place, Margaret convinced me and others that opening school was the right thing to do for our students. In retrospect, she was absolutely right.

Throughout the summer, Margaret worked tirelessly to support her teachers. She reached out to each teacher individually, talked through the decision to open, and helped alleviate their fears as best as she could. She provided the training and EdTech support so teachers could teach in a dual modality because some families opted to start the year learning remotely. She spent her weekends moving furniture and inspecting classrooms. She communicated with parents clearly, frequently, and transparently, so they knew what to expect during those opening days. As the day to welcome teachers back to campus arrived, Margaret began to isolate herself at home from her own family so she could maintain the Lower School bubble. Her division was ready to open with confidence, joy, and support. They provided a safe, healthy learning environment for students during these uncertain times.

What is Margaret's secret sauce? In short, she cares. And she cares some more. She knows what it is like to be a teacher and the importance of cultivating a culture of caring within her division. The testimonies of her teachers say it all:

- "Margaret never hesitates to jump in where she is needed. She is as comfortable and willing to act as a last-minute substitute for art class in kindergarten as she is to lead a morning meeting in fifth grade. Her office is a place where students and staff alike feel comfortable. She welcomes us, listens to us, advocates and supports, and most of all, helps all of us find workable solutions to the multitudes of issues that come up every day of the school year."

- "Margaret always puts her teachers first. She stands up for us, defends us, and calms parents down when necessary. I have always felt supported by her because I know that she has my back. When I make a mistake, she tells me that going forward I will get better/do better because she knows that I can. Her confidence in her staff makes her a remarkably strong leader."

- "Margaret builds warm, caring, and constructive relationships with her faculty in much the same way that excellent teachers strive to establish genuine and meaningful relationships with their students. She can be counted on to listen earnestly and empathetically, and there is never any question that she places students and teachers at the forefront of the decisions she makes."

- "I have always admired how Margaret greets every student and family by name. She recalls details about their lives as she asks about their day. Margaret has cultivated an environment in which students are thrilled to have a visit by the principal. It's clear she loves time spent with students, and I believe the students and families feel this."

- "I feel Margaret does everything in her power to support the students, families, and faculty alike here at our school. I am amazed at how often she puts her community before herself. I am so grateful to have a leader like her at my side."

5. Reflections on Healing Staff With Compassion

Told by the principal of a suburban public high school

An essential part of principals' work is to care for their faculty and staff. It is in being caring for them that they can be caring for the students and families they serve and be caring for one another. Over the years I have been a principal, across several schools in which I've worked, I have cared for, supported, and helped heal many teachers and staff members as they encountered individual traumas, stress, and loss. In two schools, I have tried to help heal the wounds of whole faculties and staffs. At one school, the staff was experiencing compassion fatigue after several tragedies occurred in a short period of time. Two of our former students committed suicide. The young daughter of one of our staff members died of hypothermia after wandering away and getting lost in the cold of winter. And an educational assistant who had been at the school for almost 20 years had, within a 6-month period, separated from his wife and lost his 3-year-old son in a fire while his 21-year-old son was babysitting. At the second school, the staff was traumatized from the polarizing leadership of the former principal. His toxic relationships with the faculty resulted in feelings of betrayal, mistrust, and anger. Whether an individual teacher or staff member or a whole faculty and staff, I try to promote healing with compassion and empathy, creating systems of support and communicating in a common language that promotes a caring and supportive school community for all.

One of the first things that I do to address the emotional pain of my teachers and staff members is to reach out to those who I believe are most affected. I listen to what has happened. I try to understand how they are feeling and how their circumstances are affecting them and their work. I find that the key to compassionate leadership is listening empathetically, hearing people discuss their pain, frustration, and anger without needing to minimize it based on our own discomfort. Compassionate leaders are strong enough to carry other people's pain along with them. After connecting with people one-on-one or in small groups, I have found it important to understand the depth of their pain and why they are so wounded. In the process, I hope that members will see me as someone who will ask questions and listen without judgment.

I believe that how school leaders communicate with staff is critical. To heal a staff the leader must control the narrative. I try to help my administrative teams learn early on that I need to see all correspondence that goes out to staff or to our school community until I am convinced that they are using the language that builds community and facilitates healing. I know that it probably sounds simplistic, but it is important to consistently use words such as "we are a community," "we care about each other," "we support each other," and "we are a team," and to model these words in my actions at all times. As a compassionate leader, this modeling comes naturally to me. This is who I am and always have been. I have learned that leaders who try to use such verbiage but don't model it at all will not succeed. To heal a staff requires authentic emotions, behaviors, and support. Teachers and staff members will not believe what you say if there is inconsistency between talk and action.

I've also learned that an important aspect of being a compassionate, healing leader is establishing well-working, organized systems. Disorganized systems can fuel frustration and be construed as a lack of direction and vision. If teachers and staff members have to spend time looking for information or support, they have less time to work with students and families or engage in professional development. Disorganized systems that don't work well for teachers and staff can also communicate a lack of caring by school leaders. As my team and I created systems to support teacher work, I always used the narrative that "this allows teachers more time to spend teaching and building connections with students." Language matters, and moving a staff forward in a healthy, positive, and supportive manner requires diligence in maintaining the narrative.

Communication can build communities that can help promote healing. One of the things that I have done since my first year as a principal is to send out Sunday emails highlighting the week's events. Just as importantly, I take the opportunity to thank staff and to highlight positives of the past week, particularly those related directly to teachers. At the end of the email, I always include a teacher's inspirational quote that I select to reinforce a positive message I am trying to send. Sometimes it is something fun like " I am a teacher—what is your superpower?" But often it is something more reflective like "Be the person you needed when you were young" or "Students who are loved at home come to school to learn and students who are not come to school to be loved." With every email to staff, I have the opportunity to share what is important to me as the leader of the building and what I believe to be true about the power of a great teacher to change the life of a child.

Bringing healing to an entire staff is a process that takes time, patience, and consistency. Compassionate leadership is not a style but rather a belief in how to treat people and how to facilitate growth, trust, and a sense of community. It is important to be open and honest and to be humble and prudent in one's leadership. And it is important to pay attention to the little things. Recently, I directed our custodial staff to paint over the art drawings that were above a number of doors within the school as a process of upgrading the school with fresh paint. One teacher became upset with me because a former student had created these drawings and they meant a lot to him. This teacher emailed me: "At

the least, the painter should have taken a picture of the drawings before they were painted over." I responded to her with an apology, and I owned up to my part in not notifying staff prior to my decision. She wrote back saying that in the 10 years that she had been at this school, she had never heard a school administrator apologize for anything. This meant a lot to her. Being a compassionate leader is easy when your leadership is not being challenged. But being a compassionate leader during a time of challenge calls on the leader's authenticity and communicates to staff that that their beliefs and the journey together is genuine. And that builds trust.

Teachers and support staff are human beings, and they have personal lives as well as school lives. There has been more than one occasion when a staff member was not performing up to expectations requiring a meeting to discuss the situation. The way in which such meetings are conducted says a great deal about the leadership of the principal. If the meeting starts out with a lot of "you" statements, as in, "You are not doing this—you should be doing that," the tone is one of power. A compassionate leader would approach these meetings differently, leading with questions rather than accusations. "Is everything OK? I've noticed you coming late a few days, and I know that is not typical for you." Leading in this manner has led to me to learn that teachers can be in the midst of an ugly divorce, have spouses with a recent cancer diagnosis, or have received a distressing diagnosis themselves. By approaching these meetings from a perspective of compassion, I am allowed into the staff member's world, which allows me to provide the support needed for them to be the best teacher, parent, spouse, or partner they can be. Addressing staff performance issues through compassion furthers a deeper understanding, resulting in targeted interventions, support, and improvement plans. Being a compassionate leader does not mean a lack of accountability. It means approaching leadership with human connection and understanding.

As a compassionate leader, I believe that healing a staff community and building a supportive and trusting school culture begins with having certain supports in place. At my former school, for example, I asked our social worker if she would be willing to be available to staff members in need. She agreed, so at a staff meeting, I mentioned her as a resource for teacher and staff support. I also spoke with my school counselors regularly about how they thought our staff was feeling, and I would ask them to walk the halls and check in with people. I had a new counselor tell me that he was unsure of why I had made that request, but in his walking about and asking people how they were doing, people began to share their feelings in a helpful way. As a compassionate leader, I know that I have an obligation to model compassion to others through my words and actions. I've learned that being available to staff, having an open-door policy, and asking "How can I help?" can pave the way to restoring trust and creating a culture where we all support each other.

Staff who are wounded or experiencing compassion fatigue can only give so much to students and families. The natural tendency is to isolate and protect oneself. Because we are in the work of educating students, teachers need to be emotionally available to make connections and support students in their learning. Addressing the emotional well-being of staff is therefore essential to creating a school in which all students experience academic success.

The best teachers are called to their work like to a vocation and lead with their hearts in making a difference in the lives of young people. They can be at their best when the school system that supports them is cognizant of how they are feeling and what they need to be their most healthy and successful. As a compassionate leader, I want to create pathways by which staff, particularly teachers, are able to express what they need in an atmosphere free of judgment and can find the support they need in a school that believes in the collective "we," as in "We are a family. We take care of each other. We support each other."

This Way Out—Gabriela Celio, Grade 11

6. Caring for Kids by Taking Care of Teachers

Told by two teachers at a suburban public middle school

My wife and I teach in an affluent suburban middle school. We have twin boys who attend our school. The COVID pandemic has been tough on the two of us and on our family. But it has been a disaster for many of our school's families in many ways. Our at-risk families, in particular, have experienced the loss of loved ones, financial hardships, and housing and food insecurities. This has been going on since March 2020, when we closed schools in our district and began remote learning. Our district has stepped in to help. For example, it has arranged food pickups and drop-offs for families who rely on school as a place for their children to receive two healthy meals a day. Food distribution continued during the summer and into the following fall, when schools reopened for half-day in-person instruction.

We have been lucky to participate in several projects at our school to provide support to families who needed help during the pandemic. One student of ours lost his grandfather to COVID. This man was the great grandfather of another student. He was infected with COVID by his daughter, who picked it up while working at her fast-food job. While she was sick and not working, bills piled up and put the family at risk for eviction. Then, her husband—our student's father—was hospitalized with COVID. There was a serious concern about whether he would survive. Thankfully, he's back home and almost 100 percent now. Our social workers shared the family's struggle with our faculty, staff, and school community, and together we raised $5,000 for the family to pay rent and cover other expenses. Other families in financial need received Target gift cards, so they could shop for Christmas gifts for their kids. Our social workers also used money we raised to buy grocery store gift cards, and

they rounded up winter clothes for kids who needed them.

We organized a School Spirit/Spirit of Giving Week before our winter break. We had themed outfit days such as Toasty Hat Tuesday, Ugly Sweater Wednesday, and Flannel Friday. Our building partnered with a local food pantry to collect and donate food, household goods, diapers, and formula for families in our larger community. The response from our students and their families was overwhelming. We sent more than 50 boxes of food, personal items, toiletries, and cold weather gear to the food pantry for distribution.

Before winter break we also created a video with teachers and staff members lip syncing Mariah Carey's "All I Want for Christmas Is You" and shared it with our kids on the day before break. We filmed from our own homes, held our pets on camera, included our own kids, wore Santa hats and Christmas lights, and blew kisses. I'm a big guy, a former baseball player, and I looked pretty silly. But you could see the joy in everyone's faces. In a horrible time it felt great to sing, dance, and show our kids how much we care about them.

One thing about these efforts has struck both of us—all the ideas were initiated by teachers and staff. They happened from the ground up, not the top down. Our administrators have worked hard to cultivate a strong, caring community in our school for teachers, staff, and students. They will do everything they can to support what teachers and staff try to do to care for our students and their families. When my wife and I first pitched the idea for a spirit week and the food drive to our principal, he immediately said, "Yes! I love it. Let me know what you need me to do." It is so powerful to hear from your principal a message like that—clear, unequivocal, and supportive. He could have said, "Let me think about it" and then gotten to "yes" eventually. But to hear his excitement and instant reinforcement was powerful. To top it off, he's already put these activities on his calendar for the same week next year.

7. Laura

Told by a former small-town public elementary school principal

It is hard not to fall in love with your students when you are an elementary school principal. They greet you each morning with a hug and a snaggle-tooth grin. They expect nothing in return except a nod of recognition as they head off to their classrooms each morning. I had so many of these moments as an assistant principal and principal. What I learned quickly was that those sweet smiles and big hugs often mask the pain that some children endure. As children move through the grades, I discovered that some of my students were at risk. They learned and thrived at school even though their home environments were unstable. Divorce, food insecurity, abuse, and neglect were a few of the social problems that some of my students experienced. As a principal, it was impossible to ignore, and I learned quickly that dealing with a child's social and emotional needs was my responsibility. I was hired to be the instructional leader of the school—that was the easy part. I was also a great culture builder and understood how to create opportunities for teacher collaboration, community engagement, and student voice. However, confronting a parent with questions when a child arrives at school with bruises requires a different skill set.

During my second year as principal, the mother of a first-grade student, Laura, requested a confidential meeting with the school nurse, Laura's teacher, and me. It was at this meeting that we learned that Laura, who had missed a lot of school because of her headaches and dizziness, had a diagnosis of an aggressive, terminal brain tumor. As Laura's mother sat in my office with tears streaming down her face, I realized that no graduate course had prepared me for this moment. I understood immediately that this crisis facing this single mother and child was now my greatest challenge as a school leader. I understood that my actions from that moment forward would define what kind of caring leader I wanted to be. I stood up, walked to Laura's mother, sat down beside her, and with my arm around her and looking directly in her eyes, assured her that I, along with the support staff and teachers, would provide Laura a safe and loving environment to learn and play.

When you know that a young child is in your care and that the child is unhealthy and has limited time to live, a sense of urgency overwhelms you. I woke up each morning with a feeling that I had to make whatever time Laura had at school a wonderful experience. After getting permission from Laura's mother, I met with teachers, support staff, custodians, secretaries, and bus drivers to communicate information that all staff needed to know about Laura's care. Nothing occurs in an elementary school that does not affect everyone in some way. I wanted everyone to hear the facts from me and not through hallway gossip. I was clear that I wanted Laura's experience at our school to be as normal and positive as possible. I scheduled weekly updates with the school nurse and Laura's mother. The summer break provided me opportunities to meet with health-care providers and the school counselor and to determine Laura's best second-grade classroom placement. Because the prognosis was not good, I knew that the teacher assignment would be important. I decided on a co-teaching classroom where one teacher specialized in special education. We developed an Individualized Educational Plan for Laura because of her medical condition. I scheduled a meeting with the parents of all students who would be in the classroom and explained the circumstances in case they had concerns. No one opted out. Next, I met with the students so I could explain to them that Laura was sick and might be absent a lot. The students asked many questions, and I answered them as honestly as I could without causing additional worry.

Laura had a loving and nurturing second-grade experience when she was able to attend school. The children nurtured her, helped with schoolwork, and entertained her when she played inside instead of on the playground. Their parents became a support group to Laura's mother, dropping off meals, running errands, and arranging play dates at their home. The school nurse made home visits to assist with medications and to meet regularly with home health care and hospice as Laura's health deteriorated that year. In the spring, our dear Laura passed away.

Leadership does not end when the crisis is over. Just as Laura's mother had asked to meet with me about Laura's health the year before, now she wanted to meet with me about something else. I provided my deepest condolences and asked if there was anything I could do for her. She thanked me for all I had done to provide a wonderful school year for Laura. Then she asked me, mother to mother, if I would lead the service at the church for Laura's funeral. I had no words. I said, "Yes." Two days later, I walked to the front of the sanctuary and led the service for Laura's funeral. I looked into the congregation and realized that as a community leader during a crisis, I must demonstrate empathy and care. The leader must also bring hope to those who have been through the storm. As I held the stuffed animal Laura gave to me, I accepted the responsibility for leading. I tried to provide comfort and connection with those who came to pay tribute and to mourn. I acknowledged everyone's contributions and focused on the strength of Laura and her mother and on the lessons Laura taught us about kindness, resilience, and joy. It was a difficult day. Leadership can often be difficult. I often think about this experience. I believe crisis leadership defines who we are as humans and the values that inform the decisions we make. I look back on this experience with no regrets. Compassion, care, and kindness are qualities that all school leaders need.

8. Guarding Against Sexual Misconduct

Told by the head of a small-town independent girls high school

I was sitting at my desk on a conference call for a board committee when my business manager walked in and passed me a note: "Did John Doe work here? We have a reporter calling to ask about his employment history." I felt a pit in my stomach. I immediately knew what could unfold, and I questioned myself. Am I up to this incredible responsibility?

It's one of the crisis scenarios every school leader hopes never happens but sadly has come to light in too many places where children are. John Doe was being investigated for past sexual misconduct at another school in another state, and a reporter had tracked him to the school where I had been head for less than 3 years. Because the alleged misconduct was from decades ago, I realized no current student was in imminent danger but that didn't mean we didn't face a crisis at our school.

Because of several high-profile cases of sexual misconduct at other boarding schools, my Board of Trustees and I had worked on a process for our school should such an allegation ever be raised. My team and I spent the next several days combing through records and even through old yearbooks to determine if this John Doe had, indeed, been employed and during what time frame. Per our protocols, we launched a third-party investigation, and we began work on communications.

I soon realized that what was at stake was more than determining whether or not this past employee had committed abuse and whether or not the school had passed on the proverbial lemon, so to speak. What was at stake was the care and healing of our community members from the past and the solemn work of making sure no child today or in the future suffers abuse at the hands of a school employee.

Transparency was important in telling the school community about the investigation. While the consultant we hired to oversee our investigation into our school's past set up a hotline and reached out to alumnae for whom they had received information, I found myself on calls with alumnae who shared their pain and trauma or who witnessed inappropriate behavior at the hands of John Doe. What came to light was abuse and misconduct by other teachers in other decades as well. What was revealed was the institution's turning a blind eye to red flag behaviors, falling short in response, and a faculty and student culture of not speaking up. These types of behaviors are not isolated to my school. They are found in many places where children can be found—schools, churches, community centers, camps, and so forth.

Although the statute of limitations had run out for any legal action related to John Doe or the four other credible allegations, and the administrators responsible at the time had long retired, the board and I were faced with how to acknowledge the alumnae trauma and how to help them heal. We wrote a public apology and offered support in the form of counseling to any alumni whose pain had resurfaced in the process of the investigation.

I know some survivors probably didn't feel like I did enough. I felt the incredible weight of caring for these alumnae and their pain, protecting the children currently at the school, and managing the reputational risk of the school. The latter sounds so cold, but it is part of a leader's responsibility to do it all.

The only promise I could make to our alumnae and to our current families is that we would use this painful past to make sure we put into place systems, policies, and protocols that would make it less likely for any future student to suffer abuse and misconduct. We would ensure employees who might engage in misconduct would be held accountable to the fullest extent possible. We strengthened background searches, reference checks, handbooks, and whistleblower policies. We implemented annual training for all employees on appropriate boundaries, red flag behaviors, and reporting obligations. We also now include student training on the same topic. It was important also to think about how to ensure that we nurture our culture of caring within the school community not only to help prevent future misconduct but also to dismantle norms of silence.

My hope is every day we work to empower students in primary school, in secondary school, in college, in the workplace, and in their personal relationships to accept nothing less than professional, healthy, and respectful treatment. This begins by providing students with knowledge about misconduct and abuse. It also requires that students know about the school's expectations for the adults who are charged with their education and care. It is also my hope that we have done a good enough job of empowering them that when they see or experience mistreatment and injustice, they will have the courage and confidence to speak up, take action, and demand justice.

9. One Sows, Another Reaps

Told by a former teacher in an urban secondary charter school

As a first-year teacher at a notoriously rigid urban charter school serving middle and high school students, I had my work cut out for me. On top of issuing merits and demerits, enforcing silence in hallways, and trying to navigate my way through a new city, I had to teach my students. I stumbled through the fall semester doing my best but possessing a nagging suspicion that I was failing my kids. At the end of a particularly long day, I was working the dismissal line with my principal, Mr. Volker.

Mr. Volker grew up in the neighborhood, attended the local university, and stayed to become the school's first principal. Far from being a charismatic leader, Mr. Volker could easily be described as aloof or withdrawn. But if you had the gift of learning at his side, you quickly realized that his detached demeanor belied an intense commitment to his students and teachers.

I remember standing alongside Mr. Volker as the sky spat snowflakes, unusual for early December in our part of the country. As we waved at cars leaving the parking lot, I asked him, "How are you able to do this, day in and day out? I don't think I'm making any difference to my students. . . . I never see results." Without breaking his joyless, mechanical

waving, his reply changed my whole outlook: "Mr. Maddox," he said. "One sows, another reaps." He gingerly patted me on my shoulder, and we headed inside.

Mr. Volker knew a good deal about sowing. You never saw him outside of school without at least two of our students. Whether at the grocery store, undoubtedly shopping for more than himself, attending local sporting events, or simply driving down the road, Mr. Volker was always with our students. The next day you would often see those same students in his office, head in hands, reeling after their most recent discipline infraction.

One of these students was Ashton. When Ashton was an eighth grader, his mom didn't pick him up after school one day. For one reason or another and without ceremony, she vanished. With no family in the area and facing foster care or homelessness, Mr. Volker took Ashton and his brother Marshall into his own home. Over the next three years, Mr. Volker quietly took care

Protection and Care—Emma Herzog, Grade 9

of those young men at school and after school, day after day. Most people assumed the young men were his sons, but Mr. Volker would quietly correct this misperception if given the chance. He watched out for them and worked to ensure that the whole school community embraced and supported them.

Two months before Ashton's graduation, his mom briefly appeared in a neighboring city. Without leaving a note or saying goodbye, Ashton reunited with his mom and never looked back. Several teachers and I checked in on Mr. Volker and tried to offer comfort. Although understandably shaken, he continued working for the good of the school and taking care of Ashton's brother Marshall.

What I didn't know, but what Mr. Volker clearly understood, was that school leaders—and teachers—aren't guaranteed to see the results of their efforts. It's easy to fixate on the present and overlook the long-term impact of caring for students each day, even when we don't get to see our efforts come to fruition.

10. A Million Times More

Told by a former teacher at a suburban charter high school

I stood outside the principal's door, trying to take deep breaths to calm my nerves, trying to work up the determination to knock. It was almost 5:00 pm, well past the end of the school day, but Principal Harper's light was still on. I knew he was in there, so I had no excuse not to talk to him. I was 3 months into being a math teacher, fresh out of college, and I was experiencing the first personal crisis of my career as an educator. My favorite student had been expelled for using drugs on the school bus. I was there to plead with Principal Harper on his behalf.

As a first teaching assignment, Oak Grove School was diving into the deep end. It was a charter school that served at-risk youth, many of whom had already been expelled from other schools. It was a school of last resort for many students. Our area was experiencing tremendous difficulties with gang violence, rampant youth drug and alcohol abuse, and other crimes. At Oak Grove we taught students who had seen and heard it all.

Despite feeling overwhelmed with my new teaching duties, I had connected with a few of my students right off the bat. One of them was Raymond, a tenth grader. Despite the many challenges he faced, he showed tremendous promise in our Algebra 1 class. He and I had begun working together one-on-one outside of class, and he was quickly catching up on the material he had missed during numerous suspensions at his previous school. I felt tremendously proud of him and was sure that he was in the process of turning his career as a student around.

Then, one day, Raymond wasn't in class. Other students were quick to tell me that he'd taken some drugs on the bus that morning and had been caught immediately because he began to have a bad reaction. He was already removed from my roster when I went to take attendance on the computer. Raymond had been expelled. I was devastated.

So I found myself outside of the principal's door, late that afternoon, feeling as nervous as any student ever did. "There must be some room for mercy here," I thought. "If I tell Principal Harper about all the progress he's made in class, maybe he'll give Raymond a second chance." But as a brand-new teacher, not all that much older than my students if we're being honest, I felt powerless and scared. I finally raised my hand and gave the door a few gentle raps.

"Come in!" came Principal Harper's voice. Ed Harper was on the opposite end of his career from me. He would retire at the end of that school year. He had silver hair and wore a tie, a dress shirt, and dress pants with running shoes because of his painful ankle problems. His voice was booming and commanding, but there was abundant warmth and kindness hiding below the surface. "Hey, Ron, what can I do for you?" he said as I nervously walked in.

"Principal Harper, I wanted to talk to you about Raymond." He sighed and nodded for me to continue. "It's just that . . . Raymond was making so much progress in math. And he's a great kid. I know he made an incredibly poor choice this morning, but I guess I'm asking if there's any way you might show him some mercy and let him come back to our school. I think he is on the verge of turning things around."

It's hard to describe the look I saw on Ed's face then. At first, he seemed very, very tired. There was a tremendous sadness behind his eyes, too. It looked like a tear was welling up. And there was the faintest hint of hope on his face, peeking out from behind a grim half-smile.

"Ron, there's nothing I can do. I like Raymond too. But the school district has a zero-tolerance policy when it comes to drugs. It's a condition the kids agreed to when they enrolled. My hands are tied. I literally have no choice in the matter." I felt like I was about to cry.

"But you coming down here this afternoon," he continued, "that says a lot about you as a teacher."

"That isn't why I came down here this afternoon, sir," I replied.

"I know it isn't," he said. "But listen. You're a teacher now, which means if you keep caring about kids the way you care about Raymond, your heart is going to be broken a million times more. Keep caring about them anyway."

I can't remember the rest of what was said. It may well have been me choking out a "Yes, sir, have a nice evening." But I've never forgotten that conversation. Ed Harper helped me see that when you choose to become an educator, there will never be an end to crises. Some you'll be able to help; many you won't. Nevertheless, we cannot grow weary of doing good. A great educator cares about students and their crises as much in the last year of a career as in the first year, no matter how many times you get knocked down. And a great school leader gives teachers the strength and encouragement to carry on.

---

11. Commitment to Community Health

Told by a middle-grade teacher at a K–12 independent school

Our school's director is deeply committed to the strength and health of our school's community and to the responsibility we share for each other's safety and success. This relates to the care and support we provide our students and the care and support we educators provide one another and the families of our students. Our director is also a leader in the broader community. He is an advocate for our school and for the needs and interests of children and families.

We closed our school after COVID hit in the spring of 2020. We moved quickly to online learning and, with the support and guidance of our school's leadership, maintained regular communication with our students and their families. Our director also began regular communications with students and families, being clear, open, and honest about what was known about the pandemic and its implications for our school. He assured families that we were working hard and looking out for their kids and that we were taking responsibility for the work that lay ahead. In late spring and throughout the summer, even though reopening remained uncertain, we prepared for welcoming students back to school in the fall.

An important aspect of planning was drafting the Commitment to Community Health (CCH) pledge. The CCH was a covenantal agreement of mutual support and responsibility between the school and its students and families. It sought to promote the health and safety of the school community and the health and safety of the broader community. It laid out what educators and families needed to do to open the school safely and to keep it open. Its provisions were designed to keep families healthy and safe, and by doing so contribute to the health and safety of the broader community. The principles of this agreement were contained in an oath that all teachers, staff members, and families were asked to sign.

In late July, the director introduced the CCH to families "as a way we can count on one another when school resumes" in the fall. He encouraged parents to have "a kitchen-table-type conversation, point by point, with your family." He suggested that parents print out the oath and tape it to the refrigerator. He said, "We can and must each do our part if we expect conditions out there to improve" and if we are going to be able to reopen the school safely in the fall and keep it open. The director invited any parent, teacher, or staff member who might have questions or who for some reason in good conscience might find themselves at odds with what the school was asking to come straight to him to discuss their concerns. He knew that everyone needed to be on the same page to make this work. Each teacher and staff member, and each family, was asked to sign a copy of the CCH before they would be allowed to come back to school.

The oath contained seven promises. These promises applied to parents as well as students and other family members who might live in the household. They applied to teachers and staff members and their families. It included an unbending promise to use face coverings in any public setting, wash hands frequently, and pay special attention to preventative hygiene measures; a promise to avoid nonessential travel, especially by means that place people in close confinement and to areas with known high COVID counts; and a promise to steer clear of events anywhere that bring together large numbers of people or even small numbers of people who were not adhering to CDC guidelines. The oath asked for compliance in completing daily wellness checks before school and parents were "never, ever" to send their kids to school sick. Families were asked to agree to get vaccinated for the seasonal flu to limit transmission of that illness.

Families, as well as teachers and staff, were asked to make two other important promises. Families were to commit to creating and maintaining "continuity between school and home, consistently reinforcing efforts to promote healthy choices and proven practices to limit potential COVID exposure." Families were also to "speak up, within our circles of influence, in support of these essential principles, knowing the difference each of us and all of us can make and the importance of setting an example for our city at a time of great need, one decision at a time, starting today." These promises aimed to promote health and safety both within the school's community and in the broader community outside the school.

We opened school in early September to hybrid in-person and remote instruction. I don't know of a single family, teacher, or staff member who did not sign the CCH. As the weeks went by, we adjusted to our new normal. Our director continued to communicate regularly with families, always being open and honest and continually reinforcing our commitments to community health.

In the run-up to the fall break, the director sent a letter home to families updating them on the latest health guidelines and reaffirming the promises we had made to each other. Perhaps, sensing the fatigue we were all starting to feel and growing temptations to take "just this once" risks, he introduced a moral dimension to his reminders, referring to "our categorical imperative" to keep each other safe. Anticipating the lure of travel, he provided examples of ways that families could be safe together during the break. "Picture the mini-van," he wrote, "with snacks packed, masks at the ready, heading to a sanitized rental, with plans to cook in that kitchen and avoid all crowds. Contrast that with a tour of downtown attractions and a series of dinners in indoor restaurants." He called upon our better angels. "Ultimately, we're relying on an honor system, which makes sense because we're in the company of honorable people. . . . We've embraced a high standard and an ethic, rooted in the belief that smart, caring people make wise plans and adjust according to circumstance." He concluded, "With the right kind of help, your help, one household at a time, we can make it work together."

The director's campaign continued after we returned from fall break. As we were preparing for winter break, he wrote again calling for sustained commitment and vigilance. He spoke of our success and gave credit to families, as well as to teachers and staff, for being caring of one another and abiding by our promises to one another. "Remember that Commitment to Community Health that we asked you to support back in late July? Turns out that those pledges ended up mattering quite a bit." He added, "If it sounds like we're not letting up, and if it sounds like I'm asking you to be parsimonious in managing your risk budget, well, that's true. By all means enjoy your family time in whatever distanced or mitigated way may be necessary in this extraordinary year. And look for another update next week." In all, we are doing well because of the commitments we have made to each other.

We Will Be Safe—Abe Sharfstein, Grade 5

12. Da Bears!

Told by the superintendent of a suburban public elementary school district

Remote learning comes easily to some children but not to all. In our community, many children have significant supports in place to ensure that they are successful both in school and in their personal lives. Mr. Tyler was an experienced fifth-grade classroom teaching assistant who was astute in knowing those students who did not have sufficient support.

During remote instruction, Mr. Tyler noticed that Jonathan was showing increasing levels of discomfort keeping his camera on during the lesson, and he seemed quite withdrawn during class when he did. Mr. Tyler also noticed on the screen that the room behind Jonathan was unkempt and disorganized. This differed markedly from what could be seen of other students' homes. It was clear that Jonathan's physical surroundings seemed to make him uncomfortable and embarrassed.

After class one day, Mr. Tyler asked Jonathan to stay on the virtual call, so that they could talk privately. He was artful in drawing Jonathan out to share what was bothering him. As he anticipated, Jonathan lamented that he was embarrassed by the state of his home and was greatly worried about what the other students would think of him. Mr. Tyler asked Jonathan if he had a favorite sports team, which Mr. Tyler knew would be the Chicago Bears. Predictably, Jonathan shared his love for the Bears. Together, Mr. Tyler and Jonathan searched the internet for a photo of Soldier Field, the Chicago Bears football stadium. Then, Mr. Tyler showed Jonathan how to use the image as his Zoom background.

Jonathan was elated, and his online attendance and participation soared in the weeks that followed. This one simple gesture of compassion and understanding by an adult in Jonathan's life made a real difference to him.

The way that Mr. Tyler understood and helped Jonathan reflects a broader culture of caring in the school, nurtured by the school's administrative leadership. For one, Mrs. Solter, the assistant principal, strongly preaches a philosophy about the importance of treating children with an ethic of care. She models this ethic in her work with students, faculty and staff, and families. There is no doubt that she inspired Mr. Tyler's compassionate approach to working with Jonathan and his other students. Mr. Tyler is a powerful example of how caring can spread throughout a school when leaders model the courage to connect with youngsters in compassionate ways.

13. My Zoom Isn't Working!

Told by the assistant principal of an urban public elementary school

I had begun my morning as I normally do—walking the hallways, hurrying along tardy students, poking my head into classrooms, greeting another day of learning—when Nancy careened around the corner, gasping for breath, eyes red with panic and perhaps even an errant tear. "My Zoom isn't working!"

Even under normal circumstances Nancy is a little high-strung. It's because she cares. It's because she wants to feel successful. It's because she believes she is called to be a teacher. She's told me as much, and her commitment to her students is confirmed by her work. That day, however, seemed different. Nancy was paralyzed with anxiety. How was she supposed to teach when she couldn't meet with her students? "Jerry, my Zoom isn't working!" she repeated and paused expectantly as if everything in her personal and professional life depended on my response.

Like much of the rest of the world, our school came screeching to a halt last spring because of COVID-19. As teachers were preparing their students for the final push to spring testing, schools closed, teachers quarantined, and far too many students disappeared. Teachers tried to cobble together a mishmash of Zoom calls and packets of worksheets, but it felt half-hearted and futile in the midst of the growing pandemic.

And as we were struggling with the challenges of COVID, a catastrophic storm swept through our community and destroyed our school building. The wreckage was broadcast in a seemingly endless loop by local news channels. Teachers, students, and parents confronted not only the loss of the rest of the school year but the loss of the school itself.

By the beginning of the new school year, we had moved to a temporary building, while ours was being rebuilt. Our temporary quarters were no salve though. The building wasn't ready for us. Contractors and construction crews outnumbered the school faculty. As teachers tried to unpack their materials and set up their classrooms, workers rushed to install light fixtures, routers, floor tiles, and furniture before students were slated to arrive. Nothing seemed to work. Teachers groused about the condition of the temporary building and tittered about whether this augured poorly for the eventual reopening of our rebuilt school in the midst of the ongoing pandemic.

Soon, little things became big things. A delivery of furniture during a teachers' planning period became a brouhaha involving administrators, contractors, and maintenance. A roster change aggravated long-standing grievances among teachers. A new approach to planning for literacy sparked a mutiny. A student who tested positive for COVID-19 set off ripples of distress and finger-pointing.

In such moments, I felt like pointing my finger at the teachers. "Pull yourselves together!" I wanted to say. "Act like professionals! We've got a job to do!" As frustrated as I felt, I also remembered that teachers had lost so much due to the pandemic—both professionally and personally. And they couldn't even comfort each other with hugs, cries, or mourning.

Nancy stood before me, misty-eyed and frantic. I was tempted, for a moment, to respond gruffly, to offer a dismissive solution: "Send students a message that your Zoom is down and post asynchronous assignments." That would have been all too easy. Nancy knows how to do that. In fact, that's the very thing that she proposed doing a few minutes later. I recognized in the moment that Nancy had not come to me because she did not know what to do but because she wanted someone to sit with her in the muck, to validate her feelings that this is hard, that this is unfair, that this is not what any of us signed up for.

I looked at Nancy and smiled behind my mask. I couldn't hug her. I couldn't reboot Zoom. I couldn't rebuild our school. I couldn't bring the pandemic to an end. But I could care for her.

---

14. Imagine the Possibilities

Told by the director of an education nonprofit

It was 20 days after the first case of COVID-19 was detected in the state, and the governor closed face-to-face instruction in the state's public schools. This controversial but necessary move created the same massive disruption that schools around the country had already been experiencing or would soon experience. This was an unprecedented experiment in remote learning that no one had asked for and few were prepared to undertake. There was no rule book on the steps a school should take to fair, equitable, and quality education in a virtual setting. Many of the state's schools and districts cobbled together what they could, often to simply replicate the schedule, methods, and protocols used in a brick-and-mortar setting. Attempting to apply existing protocols online laid bare a number of fundamental inequities in the traditional model of schooling to which we had all grown accustomed.

Rather than perpetuating an inadequate approach to teaching and learning, some schools used the pandemic as an opportunity for transformation. One such school was Cedar Glen Middle School. Under the leadership of principal Carol Benjamin, the school embarked on a multiweek exercise to bring students and teachers together to generate ideas about how to enable more student voice and choice and how to better address social and emotional needs of all students during and after COVID. This project took the form of a virtual design sprint that I helped support.

Using technologies such as Zoom, Mural, and Google Apps for Educators (GAFE), my nonprofit facilitated a virtual, multiweek, human-centered design process that was led by the school's students, with the support of Ms. Benjamin and two teacher leaders. Over the course of 6 weeks, more than a dozen students participated in empathy mapping; defining the problem; ideation, prioritization, and refinement of solutions; and ultimately the presentation of prototypes to the school's leadership. The work was so powerful that the school was asked to present it, along with other student-centered innovations, to the Board of Education. The initiative received statewide attention when it was featured as part of our organization's innovative program series, a multiweek project of panel discussions and storytelling events hosted by an online state education newspaper. The program series focused on educational inequities exacerbated by COVID and focused on innovations that could be adapted by schools and districts across the state to address these inequities.

Ms. Benjamin not only created an environment of collective autonomy so that everyone involved felt empowered to move their ideas forward in the time of a profound crisis. She also provided her students the freedom and trust to drive the work from start to finish. This became a perfect teachable moment, providing opportunities for students to exercise agency and voice to address an urgent problem for the entire school community. Their work became a model for other schools, demonstrating what was possible in terms of bringing student ideas to life.

In this time of crisis, when it would have been easy to exercise a command-and-control approach to expedite a response that presumed to be empathetic of student needs, Ms. Benjamin and her teacher leaders were able to use this process as a powerful way to demonstrate true caring for students, communicating at the same time respect, value, and listening and hearing. The fact that one of the early problems the design sprint highlighted was the need to better address student social and emotional needs during this time of uncertainty shows that students were also leading by caring. Students were able to explicitly see how their voice mattered and, in such a supportive environment, realize that they were not alone during what was a trying time for everyone.

Friendship—Asha Guha, Grade 5

The project's success was manifest in the fact that the students' proposals were acted upon as the school transitioned to fully remote instruction and then to hybrid learning in the fall. One of the design sprint's final big ideas was for students and teachers to use their current morning meeting time to "strengthen values within ourselves that validate individuals and build trust between staff and students along with respect for each other's boundaries." The school happily reported that, even with ongoing adjustments and challenges related to the fluid instructional context, every single student in the school had the opportunity to participate in weekly morning meeting discussion circles. Circle topics were generated from students. Circles took place for face-to-face students in their homerooms and were available to remote students via Zoom. Imagine the pride that these students felt seeing their ideas come to fruition in a way that helped their peers and allowed the school to become a model of excellence in the district and beyond!

15. On Day 2, 9/11

Told by the principal of a metropolitan public elementary school just outside of NYC

Tuesday, September 11, 2001, began as any other day for a principal heading to work. The difference for me was that it was only my second day being the leader of my own building. I remember getting out of my car that morning excited to welcome students, teachers, and parents and to start a new school year. I recall walking to the playground for morning lineups. And I remember, as everyone else has recalled, what a beautiful day it was! There was not a cloud in the sky. The temperature was perfect. And everyone was smiling and excited for the 2001–2002 school year!

As the nine o'clock bell rang, I closed the door after the last student entered the building, making sure it was locked, and made my classroom rounds to say good morning to everyone. When I got back into the main office, I remember my secretary, Doreen, saying to me, "Jeff, check the TV. Something is going on in New York." Because the internet was not what it is today, I walked to the next room over, which was the art room, and turned on the television. The news footage of the first plane, that had already hit the north tower, was on the screen. My initial thought was that of years ago, when a small plane had inadvertently struck the south tower as well. It was not until the second plane hit the tower that I and everyone else realized what was happening. I immediately got on the phone to the central office and spoke with the superintendent. Then, along with my colleagues from the other four district schools, we started to brainstorm how to handle the situation.

I walked outside for a moment to get some fresh air and heard a noise that made me nervous. When I looked up, I saw two fighter jets screaming over the top of our school, heading toward New York City. With tears in my eyes, I walked back to the office and took a drink of water. I looked at Doreen and asked her, "What the heck is happening?" I sat, stunned, and looked out the back window of the school to the large field surrounded by woods. Is this really happening? I immediately thought of the staff members who could have loved ones working in the Trade Center or in the surrounding World Financial Center buildings. I then began walking to each classroom and from the doorway called the teacher over to ask a question I could barely find the words to ask: "Do you have students with any family members who work in or around the World Trade Center?" In my mind the only answer I wanted to hear from each and every teacher was "No."

I continued around the two floors of classrooms. One by one I received the answer that I wanted to hear. Once I received an answer, I briefly told the teacher what was transpiring, and after I had an opportunity to go around to speak to everyone, if there were any teachers who felt they needed some time, I said I would cover or have an assistant cover their class. Additionally, I remember advising the staff that they were not to discuss what was happening with students as that information needed to come from home, not from their classroom teacher.

When the first tower fell, we immediately received phone calls from parents wanting to pick up their children. As parents began to pull up to the school, the look of terror on their faces caused me to hold back tears. Although at the time I had no children of my own, I felt, as did my teachers and staff, as if our students are our children. The remainder of that school day was a blur. At the end, I told all of our staff to go home and check on friends and loved ones. I then got in my car and headed home to do the same.

It was not until I got home that I started to process the number of friends and neighbors who were working either in one of the towers or in the Financial Center across the street. My neighbor to the left, Eric, and my neighbor directly across the street, Mike, both worked in the World Financial Center. My childhood friends Bob, Mike, and a few others, worked in one of the two towers. Throughout the afternoon and evening we tried to reach them through cell phone calls and text messages. As the hours went by, not hearing from them and watching from my home television, the pit in my stomach grew larger. By the grace of God, my friends and neighbors were all able to evacuate and return home safely.

As news reports continued throughout the night, all I could think about were the families who had neither heard from their loved ones nor knew of their whereabouts. I remember sitting with my wife on the couch and asking her, "What am I supposed to do tomorrow at school?" Her answer was what I expected, "Love and care for everyone there as you do every other day." And that's what I did. The next day, September 12, I made sure to check on everyone, and I made sure that students, staff, and parents all knew that our school was there in any way that anyone needed us to be.

As the days passed, it seemed that we grew stronger as a school community. As I write this story almost 20 years later, I reflect on the most important quality a building leader can have. It's not a skill, professional knowledge, or experience. It's empathy. It is the most important thing we can express and impart to our students and our fellow educators. The daily practice of putting the well-being of others first has a uniting effect in our relationships, in our friendships, and on the way we treat each other. Anything other than this will never allow you to get through the challenging times you will inevitably face.

16. Responding to the Crises[76]

Told by the principal of an urban public high school

Each year, we experienced shootings in the community surrounding our school that affected our students tremendously. Most commonly, our students were the victims of shootings that resulted in injuries and even death. One of our students from the class of 2011 was killed, one student was tragically injured and left as a quadriplegic, and many others were shot but not permanently injured. Each time a tragedy like this happened, it threw our school's culture into a tailspin, and we had to figure out how to best handle it. It also personally and deeply affected me and our entire staff. These were students who we had spent 4 years working with,

---

[76] Reprinted with permission from Smylie et al. (2021).

cultivating, and shaping. I learned to make sure my school cell phone was next to me each night as I went to sleep. When it rang in the middle of the night, I knew exactly what the call would be. The only thing I did not know was who.

When I received the call in the middle of the night on a Friday that a senior, Tony Franklin, was killed, I was inconsolable. He had brought his college acceptance letter to school on Thursday. It was the most excited I had ever seen him. I had the rest of the night and early Saturday morning to draft my plan to handle staff and student emotions and put the crisis intervention plan in place. I waited until 8:00 a.m. to begin calling my staff to tell them personally. I heard the pain and heartbreak for what could have been in each of their voices as I delivered the news. I also called a staff meeting Monday morning for 7:00 a.m. so that I would have the opportunity to inform our staff of the crisis plan for students. At the Monday morning meeting, we all cried together before the students began arriving. Because Tony was a senior, as each senior student walked into our building, we ushered them into our auditorium. Our senior teachers were there, along with the district's crisis intervention team, and we all sat around, cried, hugged, and talked about Tony. It was a free space where students had the opportunity to feel and express emotions, and as students expressed their sadness and recuperated enough to feel prepared to leave, they exited the auditorium and moved on to their classes. At Tony's funeral, I spoke to the crowd that filled the church about what we, the whole school, loved about Tony. I was extremely proud that 90 percent of my staff was in attendance and at least half of our student body. Despite all of the problems we faced as a staff and a school community, we were there in solidarity to show our unity, and that meant a lot to everyone.

School staff and students rallied like this in all of our crises. When Jackie Watkins, another senior from the class of 2011, was shot in the neck and paralyzed, most of our staff went to the hospital to see her. In fact, when I told the nurses that I was Jackie's principal, they told me, "I want my children to go to your school. So many of your teachers and staff have been here to show their love. I've never seen anything like it." Months later, when Jackie was finally released from the hospital but confined to a bed and wheelchair and unable to return to school, my teachers went to her house to give her lessons so that she could still graduate. And she did.

Our students were often the victims of violence, but unfortunately sometimes they were also the perpetrators of violence. During the course of our first 4 years, many of our students were charged with crimes, and many times we experienced police officers coming into our school, entering our classrooms, and arresting students in front of their peers. This was shocking to me and to the staff at first, but we learned that this too was a reality that we had to deal with. For example, one of our smartest senior boys was arrested right out of his precalculus class and ended up facing 20 years in prison for attempted murder. Other students were apprehended at school for home invasion burglaries, armed robberies, muggings, drugs and weapons charges, and other crimes. Each time something like this happened, we had to work to rebuild our culture. Some students would find these events funny, or at least they responded in such a manner, perhaps to masquerade their true emotions. This could trigger angry reactions from other students, and we had to implement a response system to handle the conflicts that inevitably surround these issues.

Teachers also experienced a variety of emotions when things like this happened. I saw teachers lose hope in the work they were doing, feeling like they as individuals and we as a team were not having the impact on students' lives as we had hoped—and even that our work was futile. I also experienced teachers take a negative outlook on students, viewing them all as criminals or potential criminals. But for every negative experience, we had 10 positive ones, and these are the messages we constantly had to remind our staff and students of to give them the stamina to continue their work and their efforts.

17. A Deadly Threat

Told by the principal of an urban public high school

I was principal of a high school with a student enrollment that was 85 percent Mexican American and 15 percent African American. The Mexican American and African American students lived in two adjoining communities that generally did not get along well. There were sometimes violent clashes between them. Most occurred among the adults of these communities, and gangs were prevalent. Luckily, Mexican American and African American students generally got along well within the school.

As is the case in many urban areas, the African American students had to ride a city bus or walk through the Mexican American neighborhood to get to our school and to return home. Sometimes there would be name-calling and occasional skirmishes. Sometimes a few African American students would holler racial epithets out the bus windows, thinking they were safe, and the Mexican American students would chase down the bus, board it, and fights would ensue. Most of the year, nothing serious would happen, and there were no devastating outcomes of these confrontations.

However, in my second year as principal, one of my new African American freshmen, Brandon, started racial name-calling a young Mexican American student, Miguel, as he walked home through Miguel's neighborhood.

Brandon evidently had been doing it repeatedly and loudly. Miguel had asked several older members of a Mexican gang not to bother Brandon because he was a special education student and did not know how to control himself and behave appropriately. Our special education case manager became involved after Brandon's grandmother reported that she was worried about his behavior and his safety. Brandon kept calling Miguel racist names. And before long the gang members had had enough of it.

One Friday morning I was visited separately by several of my students, each of whom relayed a message that Brandon was in danger. Gang members had said that if he came through their neighborhood again, they would kill him. I went to the station where our school police officers were assigned and asked if gang members were prone to delivering mysterious messages to people as warnings. I then explained what had been happening and the messages that I was receiving. The police officer I spoke to responded that the message was probably sent by the gang and that the young man was indeed in danger.

I rushed back to my office, called the district's Security Department, and asked for assistance. I was told to start a Student Protection Protocol and call another high school—one that receives

Shark—Paul Fortunato, Grade 5

students in danger, talk to the principal, and ask for permission to do an immediate emergency transfer for Brandon to attend that school. Fortunately, Brandon did not come to school that Friday. I called his grandmother and told her we had done an immediate transfer to another school and he was never to return to our school because his life was in danger. The grandmother was grateful.

I am glad that these gang members had sent warnings to me through my students so that I could find a way to save Brandon. But the whole situation, the gangs, the violence are terrible. I'll do everything I can to help keep my kids safe.

18. Start Simple

Told by a teacher at a suburban K–12 independent school for
students with learning disabilities

In early March of 2020, talk of COVID-19 was beginning to seep into my school. We had heard news stories about schools in China that had been doing virtual learning for weeks. "Can you imagine if we had to do that?" Given that all of our students have learning disabilities, it seemed impossible that we could adapt our teaching to video chats and iPad apps. No matter, we thought. It would never happen here.

Within days, we found ourselves sitting in a faculty meeting being told that we would not be returning to school after spring break. We would be distance learning instead. The anxiety in the room was palpable. However, the tension slowly began to ease as our Lower School division head, Dr. Byars, explained her plan. Her message was clear: we will start simple. There would be no synchronous instruction during the first 2 weeks. We would begin with asynchronous assignments in one subject per day. Over the first 2 weeks, we would gradually introduce additional subjects until all of the core academic areas were included. In the third week, we would introduce synchronous teaching over Zoom, again beginning with the most critical subjects. Our virtual learning schedule would continue to expand until it approximated a full school day.

This gradual approach allowed us all to breathe a sigh of relief. "We can handle one or two assignments per day," we thought. Then it turned out that we could handle three or four assignments. And when it came time to add Zoom sessions, we found that we could handle that too. Each step was within our reach. This was true not only for teachers but also for students and families. Like teachers who were struggling to adapt, students also needed to gradually ease into the idea of learning at home. A "zero-to-60" switch to virtual learning would have overwhelmed them. With a slow and steady approach, they were able to accomplish more than I ever could have imagined.

I was especially grateful for Dr. Byars's leadership. Some schools were refusing to provide any services to students with disabilities for fear that they might not be able to fulfill the requirements of their IEPs. There was even talk of waiving legal protections for these students. In many cases, the message seemed to be, "We don't know how to serve these students virtually, so we won't even try." It broke my heart to see so many students written off, and I was so grateful that my school's leadership was committed to giving our best effort for our students.

I also saw many teachers at other schools drowning in unrealistic expectations. Teachers with their own families to care for at home were being required to sit on Zoom for nine straight hours every day, trying to implement a completely new way of teaching with no training or support. Once again, I was grateful for Dr. Byars's measured approach, grateful that she didn't throw us into the deep end but instead let us wade in slowly. I can't imagine how difficult it must have been for her to strike the right balance between providing our students with the services that they desperately needed and making sure that neither students nor teachers were overwhelmed. Thanks to her caring leadership, we were able to tackle what seemed impossible in a way that exceeded all of our expectations.

19. Keeping Connected With the Kids

Told by the principal of a suburban public elementary school

As COVID spread and we transitioned to remote learning, I sensed the anxiety of students, teachers, and families around what this next little while would be like. Not far beneath the surface of that unease was a realization that all the habits, customs, rhythms, and routines we knew and counted on would be disrupted. I knew that for myself and for our school community, finding things we could still do that in some way resembled the way we would have done them was going to be important.

On the first day of remote learning and every day thereafter for the next 2½ months until the school year ended, I video recorded the morning announcements and emailed them to families and students. From the "ding, ding, ding" of the resonator bells, to the Pledge of Allegiance, to birthday wishes, right up to the closing—"Let's make it a great day! The power to do that is yours!"—it was all as it had been before, with one exception. Where a joke or

two had been a Friday ritual, finding reasons to laugh would be more important than ever. So a joke each day, collected from students via a Google Doc, became the new norm. It was heartwarming to hear how something so short and simple became an anchor for families struggling to keep kids connected and make remote learning work.

Although we had undertaken One School, One Book adventures before, it also seemed that having that common reading journey while we were apart could be another anchor to an otherwise disorienting arrangement. Each day I read and recorded the chapter of a book and sent the file to students and parents via email. They could listen to my reading during the day or, like many families, have their children read the chapter along with me as a bedtime story. The first book, *Almost Super*, is a story about a family where the kids have to find a way to be heroic and then find a way to use their

Screen to Heart—Harper Cleghorn, Grade 6

superpowers to save the day. After I recorded a few chapters, teachers began to volunteer, and soon students were treated to a variety of readers. When we finished *Almost Super*, we went on to other books.

One more routine we not only maintained and actually did more of was getting together—all of us, students and teachers. Where we might have had an occasion for an all school assembly once every few months, we now began gathering via Zoom every few weeks. The power of seeing each other, and seeing *everyone* across the pages of 25 thumbnails, cannot be overstated. The greetings, the smiles, the waves—seeing entire families gathered in front of their cameras became a strong and fortifying reminder that we were still a school even though we could not be at school.

20. Prioritizing Our Students

Told by the principal of an urban public elementary school

Before remote learning, the days were chaotic. Teachers, staff, and families were frightened by the novel coronavirus. The state and district were unprepared for the pandemic and the decision to send students home to be taught there remotely by teachers. So many questions swirled: How deadly was the virus? How did it spread? How would teachers teach via the internet? A million unknowns flew from every direction, and no one had answers. The district said to pause everything, and it would come up with a plan. Two school days before remote learning was to begin, the teachers and I had to answer one question: If students didn't have devices at home, could schools send Chromebooks with home students? Although the district directed us not to send home devices, we said yes. Our children's learning was at stake.

It was Friday, and the district was going to start remote learning the following Tuesday. We had one school day—Monday—to prepare, but we also had the weekend. The assistant principal and I turned to our teachers, who knew our students individually. They had great, positive relationships. They would know which students had devices at home and which didn't. So we threw together a quick e-survey to ask teachers over the weekend to identify which students we would need to send Chromebooks on Monday.

By Monday morning, we knew the exact 47 students who needed Chromebooks. The assistant principal, in a Herculean effort, prepared them for transit, adding a short letter of explanation to parents. I added usage expectations. They were delivered to students' homes that day in defiance of the district.

The district had made it clear that no devices should go home until a centralized plan had been developed. We knew that we would be excluding our students from learning if we had waited for approval from the district. And we had no idea if a forthcoming plan would be adequate for our students. For us, it was an easy decision. So, we sent home those 47 Chromebooks. By the end of spring, we had sent home another 50 Chromebooks.

None of this would have been possible if our teachers had not developed such strong relationships with our students and through those relationships come to know about their home lives and tech needs. And because of their unwavering commitment to our students, we were able to marshal the delivery of Chromebooks in a day to keep all students connected with school, each other, and their learning. We took the risk of being disciplined by the district for insubordination because we wanted our students to stay connected.

21. A District Office Caring for Teachers

Told by a district coordinator of a suburban public school district

"We must respond now" was the tone of the messaging as our district moved to quickly help teachers address the unprecedented demands being made on them during the COVID-19 pandemic. These demands included teachers needing to meet the needs not only of students in their classrooms but also of those learning from home. They included increasing demands at home. And they included demands that teachers attend to their own physical and mental well-being. My district's leadership took these needs seriously.

Only a few months into the pandemic, district leadership was consistently hearing how their teachers were wearing down. They needed more time to do their work and to take care of themselves. Often a district as large as ours would take months if not a full year to change the master schedule, and it would likely wait for a clean break—such as a change of semester or a summer break—to implement change. The COVID crisis did not allow for waiting. The call went to the school board in the middle of the semester and made its case so clearly and convincingly that the board immediately granted the unusual request to insert multiple early-release days into the master schedule so that teachers could pick up dozens of desperately needed hours to plan, prepare, and manage their course loads as well as to attend to their families and to their own physical and emotional health.

Getting board approval for the new measure was only the beginning. The real care of district leadership shone through in the implementation of this new measure. It was clear from the start that the purpose of early release days was to relieve teacher workloads, not make space for other district, school, or department initiatives. And district leadership stood behind that purpose and enforced it on all of our campuses. Teachers were given protected time to address their own personal and professional needs. Department,

campus, and district leaders committed to not call meetings or make any other demands on this time. So far, this initiative has been widely supported and appreciated by teachers.

District leadership also made a commitment to promote teachers' mental health through an intense campaign of individual contact and support. Leadership's biggest concern was teacher burnout. Our schools are grouped into regions, and there is a district-level leader responsible for each region. One regional leader scheduled one-on-one meetings with every one of her teachers before the school year began. Although this took considerable time, she understood that personal contact was absolutely necessary for teachers' mental health. These individual meetings reflected the priority the administration placed on the care and well-being of teachers.

Weekly half-day visits to every high school campus were scheduled with the intent of deepening relationships with teachers beyond supervision and evaluation. These visits often included conversations that identified teachers' needs and aspirations that probably would not have come up in a formalized setting. The overall impact of these visits was stunning. At the end of what was arguably one of the most difficult terms teachers experienced, the most common feedback was that they felt supported. They wanted this sort of personal communication and interaction to continue, and they were grateful to district leaders who were providing such support.

Having been a teacher recently myself, I understand what sorts of demands are facing the teachers I am charged with supporting. Whereas a normal start of year asks more than enough of any teacher, the uncertainty of this year was only adding to the challenges teachers were facing. It was my aim to do whatever I could to help mitigate these challenges no matter how large or small the task might be.

I visited schools regularly. Each time I went into a classroom, I asked "How can I help?" I spent time installing computers in a classroom, sorting student IDs, substituting for multiple teachers, and monitoring hallways, among other things. None of these activities are part of my job description, but my sole purpose was to be helpful.

What mattered a lot wasn't the amount of work that I tried to take off of teachers' shoulders, it was the approach I took. I wanted to show teachers with my actions that I cared for them. I knew that they were working extremely hard. While I took as many steps as I could to help, I also took moments to check in with them, ask them how they were doing, and learn about the challenges they were facing both in and out of school. I prioritized making human connections.

As I reflect on this trying period, which is still ongoing, the idea that rings truest to me is the vital importance of relationships. It is something we preach to our teachers all the time—they must develop strong, supporting, caring relationships with their students to have the greatest possible impact. Education is such a human endeavor; it requires that we look beyond curricula, pedagogies, organization, and management into the everyday experiences of our students. The same can, and must, be understood about our teachers as well.

22. We Need to Talk About Sarah

Told by a teacher at an urban independent K–12 girls school

Fighting back tears of frustration and exhaustion, I made my way down the hallway to the Upper School head's office. It was a cold winter day in the middle of my second year of teaching, and I needed help. One of my advisees had lied to me about her missing work for chemistry class, and I was at my wit's end. I went to Catherine, the Upper School head, and said, "We need to talk about Sarah."

My first interaction with Sarah happened a year before, about halfway through her freshman year. I was a first-year teacher and assigned to a freshman advisory. Although Sarah was not in my advisory group, I had heard a lot about her because her mother was sick with cancer. At this small all-girls school, the faculty are often aware of the challenges facing students. That morning during a class meeting, I was standing in the back of the room when I saw Sarah crying. I pulled her into the hallway and asked if she was all right or wanted to talk. She said that she did not want to talk but wanted me to sit with her for a few minutes. We sat in silence as she continued to cry. I wasn't sure how best to help Sarah, but I knew she needed support and care.

I didn't have much more interaction with Sarah during the rest of her freshman year. However, the faculty, administration, and her fellow classmates surrounded her with love and care when her mother passed away right before Christmas. Weeks before her death, Sarah's mother was able to see Sarah give a senior speech, an important tradition at the school. Sarah, who was given a special opportunity to deliver this speech as a freshman so her mother could attend this rite of passage, stood up before the entire school community and told them about the love, care, and relationship she had with her mother. It was beautiful and devastating, knowing what lay ahead for Sarah in the wake of her mother's death.

As I was packing up my classroom for the summer break that year, I was stopped by the director of Learning Services and the Upper School head to talk about assigning me to a sophomore advisory.

They said that Sarah would be in my group and that she would need a lot of attention and support. The second half of the year had been difficult for Sarah. In addition to dealing with her grief, she also struggled with poor executive functioning and other learning differences. She had barely passed most of her classes. Her father, who was incredibly supportive of the school, had a fraught relationship with Sarah, and his wife's death had widened the gap between him and his daughter. He looked to the school to provide the support to help Sarah get through her high school years. They had discussed having leaders at school, including her advisor, take on the more active role of monitoring her work and grades, so the father could concentrate on repairing their relationship.

I entered that next school year with excitement, but also with some trepidation. In addition to seeing Sarah every morning for advisory, she was enrolled in my U.S. history class. What I began to see was a bright and creative young woman. She was a beautiful artist and an analytical thinker who was quick to see contradictions and complexities in history class. It was soon clear that she brought this analytical lens to all aspects of her life.

While Sarah started the year out strong and wanting to have a different experience than her freshman year, challenges and new crises emerged quickly. What was clear was that her sophomore year would be the "year of firsts," where she had to cope and manage the first milestones without her mother. When Sarah would stop turning in her work for classes or withdraw from the advisory group, it was a clear sign that she was struggling with a new reminder of her loss. Her mother's birthday, the anniversary of her death, and Sarah's own birthday were all colored by her grief and longing. Sarah and I had built a good rapport over the first few months of the school year. She learned to trust me and could be honest about her academic and emotional challenges. When these issues emerged, we would work together to create a plan for her school assignments but also work

with the school counselor and her father to get her the emotional support she needed.

We had worked out this routine by winter, but suddenly something changed. Sarah's chemistry teacher reached out to say that she was missing a number of assignments that she had promised to turn in that day. The next morning during advisory, I asked Sarah about the assignments, and she said that she had turned them in the previous afternoon. Our relationship had been built on mutual trust and respect, so I gave her the benefit of the doubt. When I received another email from the chemistry teacher that afternoon with the news that in fact, Sarah had not turned in her work, I was furious. I had spent my planning periods the day before tracking down Sarah's teachers and trying to help her organize her work, and she had lied to me.

That's when I realized that I could not continue to support Sarah academically on my own and found myself again in Catherine's office. The challenges that we had been addressing separately needed a more comprehensive and holistic plan. Catherine listened to my concerns and suggested that we bring Sarah in for a meeting. We called her father to tell him of our plans, and he shared that Sarah had just learned in a family therapy session that her mother had been sick for the past 5 years, not just a few months like she had previously thought. She felt betrayed by both her father and mother. She felt she had not been given the time or opportunity to truly process her mother's illness. Suddenly, Sarah's change in behavior made more sense. Her anger, her deflections, and ultimately her grief were still raw.

When Sarah came to meet with us, we let her explain what had been going on. As she described her feelings of sadness and betrayal, it was clear that Catherine and I, along with other key leaders in the school, would need a community approach to help Sarah through this latest crisis. However, Catherine also believed that Sarah needed some tough love and that we needed to make it clear to her that dishonesty was not going to work moving forward.

It was one of the toughest conversations I've had with a student, but I felt supported by the leaders at my school. It set in motion a more comprehensive plan to support Sarah through her sophomore year. I partnered with the Learning Services director and the school counselor to have weekly check-ins with Sarah about both her academics as well as her emotional and mental health. We pulled in all of Sarah's teachers. I met every few weeks with them to better understand Sarah's behavior and engagement in class. Sarah and I checked in every morning during advisory, and she knew that I expected her honesty, even when it was hard or she had fallen behind. We rebuilt that trust, and she knew that I had high expectations for her but that I was also in her corner and would support her no matter what. Catherine and I met with Sarah's father so that he would worry less about her grades and more about mending and rebuilding his relationship with his daughter.

Over time, Sarah came out of this dark period and began once again to engage with her peers, teachers, and others at the school. Although there were still highs and lows, particularly around key milestones and anniversaries that her mother would not be part of, Sarah knew that she had her school community behind her. Catherine's leadership and the willingness of the other adults in the school to partner with me to support Sarah made me feel more confident in my role as an advisor. This ultimately led to better outcomes, not only for Sarah but also for other students who were struggling with mental health or other family challenges.

I left the school at the end of that year and moved to be closer to my family. During our last advisory meeting, Sarah came up to me with a small plant made out of clay that she had made during her free time in art class. She had also written a short note, which said, "Thank you, Ms. Read. You made this year just a little more fun." I was incredibly touched by this gesture and will always remember Sarah's resilience and growth.

Like a plant that needs good soil, sunshine, and water to grow, students also need a team of support to work through the challenges that life brings their way. While Sarah continued to slip up at times as she processed her grief as well as confronted other challenges that came with being a teenager, working with Sarah taught me that little by little, a community approach to supporting a student in crisis can make a positive, lasting impact.

Dark Place—Jasmine Wood, Grade 12

23. Coping With Loss

Told by the chief administrator of a rural charter school

Our school had developed and continuously refined remote learning practices for several years, so when we were forced into weeks-long remote learning due to the coronavirus pandemic, our teachers, administrators, and support staff felt well prepared to expand the same remote learning environment to which we had all become accustomed. But after only a week of operating this model on a daily basis, our teachers noticed several disturbing patterns in student behavior that we hadn't seen in the past.

Students who were at least moderately engaged in school failed to connect to their online classes each day. At the same time, teachers would log on as scheduled only to discover that students were already there conversing with one another about their new reality. Comments from students like "I have to leave class now to watch my little sister," "I miss you, Ms. Smith," and "I can't wait to see you guys again, man" became more common. And then it happened.

I can safely say that the most difficult crisis an educator will ever face is the loss of a student. Three weeks into the extended remote learning, our beloved, ultra-cool, funny, smiling Manny took his own life. Our entire community was simultaneously shocked and utterly devastated.

What signs were there that we didn't see? Would he still be alive today if we weren't operating remotely for so long? If we hadn't been so focused on our own struggles to make sense of the daily chaos of the pandemic, would the story have been different? If we weren't so hell-bent on monitoring assignments and academic performance, would we have seen more clearly the true extent of the emotional toll of the pandemic on our students and staff?

After the initial shock began to subside, our leadership team and faculty made the decision to stop instruction for 3 days to rethink how to better support students and each other. Never again would any student go more than a day without some form of personal interaction with a staff member. We would find ways to make it safer and more acceptable for students and staff alike to talk candidly about their individual and collective struggles, experiences, and celebrations *during the school day.* Expanding our culture of care became the utmost priority.

We reopened days later with a multifaceted approach to holistic support. Among the new strategies we implemented was our daily advisory period for all high school students, with fully integrated social-emotional learning (SEL) activities as a core component. Advisory quickly became a vital platform for students to grieve and grow together with their peers.

For our middle schoolers, we created standalone SEL courses as electives and were intentional in making sure that our male and male-identifying students could connect with male facilitators. Whereas middle school students can be less than eager to share their feelings with peers, the strategy proved effective at normalizing for students positive coping behaviors to help them deal with the uncertainties of COVID in healthy ways.

Whenever a student was absent for more than a day, a counselor would call the student's parents to explore difficulties and put in place strategies to help families reconnect. When a message wasn't returned or there was no working number on file, counselors made home visits. When issues with food, supplies, or internet connectivity surfaced, we banded together to address them. We weren't perfect, but we never gave up.

We also put in place similar measures for staff. Our administrators scheduled regular one-on-one conversations with each teacher to foster positive mental health. During post-observation conferences, administrators would intentionally ask teachers, "How are you doing personally through all of this?" and "What can we (leaders) do better to support teachers and students?" Based on these conversations, we revised our operating budget to set aside substantial funds for a Sunshine Committee to identify things we could do to boost morale, like a daily coffee bar, monthly breakfasts, and staff recognitions.

We created a yearlong leadership development series to help our grade-level leads, administrators, and department heads bring out the best in others.

I'm often asked, "What improvement strategy have you found to be most effective for high-poverty schools, rural schools, urban schools, STEM schools, STEAM schools . . ." and so forth. The answer is simple: start with a culture of care!

24. Bring Your Dog to Work Days
Told by the principal of a suburban public high school

This is a story of how a simple idea ended up changing the environment of an entire high school.

It all began when our school social workers called a local shelter to bring adult dogs and puppies to school during final exam week to help reduce student stress. Then it spread to *two* shelters worth of dogs. It still was not enough for the amount of staff and students who wanted to visit the dogs. There were some great photo ops with kids and puppies rolling around the ground of our media center, smiling and happy. "Stress relief week" with dogs quickly became a tradition before final exams.

This continued for 2–3 years, until the year the shelters couldn't make it. Because the best ideas are born out of being in a pickle, our social workers and counselors asked if I would bring my dog to school. This would not be the first time. Because I work year-round, I would bring my dog to work with me once in a while during winter or summer breaks to walk around the empty building and football field. One year, my dog was my date to the homecoming parade. Our social workers also asked another teacher who had a trained support dog for his son to bring that dog, too. So we did.

It worked out well, but the dog–student ratio was too high. The next semester, two more

teachers asked if they could bring their dogs to school during stress relief week. By the next semester, six staff members were bringing their dogs. Because they kept their dogs with them while they taught, it was like a whole bunch of stress relief every period for the students in their classes. On these days, other teachers would ask to borrow my dog so that students could read to him or so that our most profoundly disabled students could interact with him.

I quickly noticed that students were in better moods and so were the adults. The dogs brought smiles to everyone's faces. Students who were otherwise quiet and reserved would stop to pet the dog and then begin to tell me stories about their lives or family.

I never did check with my superintendent or district administrators to see if any of this was OK. I took a chance, and it paid off. After these experiments, they would see the impact dogs were having on our students and staff. They soon found themselves firmly in the "This is a great idea!" camp. *Whew!*

I began to think about how we could have a dog dedicated full time to the school. I researched and talked to other schools that had brought in therapy dogs on a limited basis, but I knew I wanted something more robust. I formed a plan and approached the superintendent with a detailed vision of having two full-time dogs in the school. Both would be dogs owned by staff members, but the school would pay a small monthly stipend to the owners for some upkeep costs such as grooming, dog food, training, and so on. In return, the staff members would bring their dogs to school. One would "live" during the day in our student services office with a counselor or social worker. This dog would be available to students in crisis or available to participate in group meetings with students. The other dog would "live" with me in the main office and be the general all-around dog for petting or for teachers to "reserve" for a particular class period. The Board of Education agreed to let us try this, and we got two puppies!

Then COVID hit, and the building shut down. The school was empty, and I worked from home the rest of the school year. When the puppies were old enough, we began bringing them to the school to get acclimated with the new environment. We slowly started to socialize them with the small number of staff who were still working

in the building. We did this all summer, and when staff came back for opening in-service week, they got to meet our new helpers.

My idea was to use the dogs to help our students cope and relieve stress. Without students in the building, it was the adults who ended up needing the dogs the most. During the fall semester, we toggled between remote and in-person learning, while our staff and teachers worked full time from the building. They would take the dogs for walks, and they began to keep boxes of dog treats in their offices or on classroom desks. One support staff member told me, "The best thing to happen in all of 2020 is these dogs." The dogs are now pictured as official staff members in our yearbook, and we are looking forward to the day when our hallways will be full again with students. Until then, the dogs will bring comfort to our staff members who have never experienced stress like this before. Sometimes, going with your instincts and sticking to what you believe is right pays off in the end.

25. "With Every Difficulty, There Is Relief"

Told by a department chair of an urban PreK–12 independent school

As an effort to promote the inclusion of students in our school community, a small group of seventh- and eighth-grade girls took responsibility for the inspirational quotes bulletin board. Typically, students displayed a Bible verse about generosity or kindness toward others because the girls in charge of the board all attended church together in this predominantly conservative Christian community.

One week, after asking a teacher if it would be OK, a Muslim student proposed a verse from the Qur'an: "So, verily, with every difficulty, there is relief (94:5)." The girls in charge printed the quote and affixed it to the board as the only inspirational quote for that week. While visiting campus, a parent of a young child saw the verse, took a picture, and posted it to social media claiming

that it was "outrageous" that students were being asked to consider the quote as inspiration. "The school is a Christian school!" the parent wrote, mistakenly characterizing the school. "They are asking our children to learn from the KORAN!" Before long, the post received more than 100 comments, both in support of the parent and in support of the students.

The principal of the middle school, Mr. Gordon, was in a tough place. A Jewish man himself (more spiritual than practicing), he understood the importance of exposing students to faiths outside of Christianity. For a few years he had been encouraging teachers to consider diversity within their curricula. He was keenly aware that teachers were upset that a student matter had been posted publicly on social media and had gained quite a bit of traction in the community.

Mr. Gordon talked to the students in small groups throughout the week, while school board members held meetings to consider diversity on campus. To stop the gossip, Mr. Gordon had the middle school faculty sit in a circle during the next faculty meeting to openly discuss the matter. Mr. Gordon began by sharing his own feelings, setting aside briefly his role as an administrator and decision maker and leaving space for teachers to share their own feelings in return. After this initial conversation, Mr. Gordon came back to the next week's faculty meeting to report on how meetings with the board and other students were progressing.

Although most of these conversations were not shared in any public forum, nearly every member of the middle school community was touched in some way. Some families felt as though only the Bible should be shared on campus because the vast majority of students were Christian. Others felt that it wasn't a bad idea to share other faiths. A few felt that any religious text had no place on campus.

At the end of the day, the board quietly met in an emergency session to amend the school handbook in two ways, both in response to this incident. The first change was an affirmation of diversity for the campus, stating that all religions were welcome. The second change was a social media policy for families. The policy now reads that families should not share posts that portrayed the school in a negative light. If there were disagreements, parents and students were asked to share them with administration rather than spread them on social media platforms.

While this controversy was riling up the community, Mr. Gordon was considering his next career move. We knew that he had his eye on other positions and that he was interviewing candidates to be his own replacement. The eventual top pick was a woman who responded similarly when told about the incident: the need to protect students and faculty from public broadsides was top of her mind. To her, a commitment to religious diversity, as supported by the board, was essential.

---

26. Tone Deafness

Told by a counselor at a suburban Catholic high school

There is perhaps not an effective word to capture the reality of the summer of 2020. Referring to it as a period of "social unrest" fails to capture the centuries-long oppression of people of color and Black individuals and communities in particular. Social unrest occurs in many forms for many reasons, and this was not simply social unrest. A confluence of factors that both exacerbated and highlighted inequities in our country led to an amplification of voices that had been silenced and some increasing awareness among privileged populations. This backdrop of crisis is relevant to this story of a small, southern suburban Catholic high school that failed spectacularly to respond to the death of George Floyd. In the midst of this failure, one school leader examined her own privilege and

led the charge to rectify the school's and diocesan district's tone deafness.

Following George Floyd's murder by law enforcement and the eruption of protests—including some in our school's adjacent city—our principal knew that as a community leader, he could not stay silent. He drafted an email that he hoped would satisfy his constituencies, a large component of whom were semi-rural whites. However, in trying to ensure that no feathers were too ruffled, he missed an important opportunity to take a stand against oppression and to educate those who choose ignorance of systemic racism. The email to the entire community expressed some concern for the well-being of individuals of color but also casually defended police officers. It was nuanced when nuance was not warranted. Backlash ensued. A caucus of alumni submitted an open letter to the school community calling the response inadequate and requesting that the school do much better.

In the midst of this experience, the director of ministry, a caring school leader and, by virtue of her position, a voice for the marginalized, recognized that she too had missed an opportunity. Despite having read the principal's email before its distribution, she did not anticipate the pain and distrust it would cause. Reeling from her oversight, she took action, galvanized by her own self-reflection.

Leveraging her relationships and her capacity to create genuine connection, she reached out to student leaders, was candid with her own and the school's struggle to respond effectively, and worked collaboratively to create safe spaces for conversation. Delving into antiracist theory and practice, she sought to bring students and staff into the work with her and create opportunities for self- and system evaluation. Being in a predominantly white school in a predominantly white area, she knew she had to establish support for and authentic connections with her school's small number of families and students of color. Through conversations, feedback requests, focus groups, and forums, she spearheaded an initiative to provide care and educate simultaneously.

Her transformative work happened only because she was willing to examine her own thinking and behaviors and be open to acknowledging her own racial biases and areas of ineptitude. She did not build care, safety, and growth by plowing forward confidently. Instead, she recognized care as more powerful than ego and chose to connect through humbling truthfulness.

27. Centering on Community

Told by the former community school coordinator of an urban public elementary school

The spring of 2015 was a scary time to be a resident of Baltimore, Maryland. As an educator, my fear was amplified. On April 19, a young Black man named Freddie Gray died after injuries sustained while in police custody following his arrest. Unlike so many stories of police brutality against Black people, this case—at the start—was not so clear-cut. As news circulated about Freddie's encounter with the police, his "rough ride" in a police van, and eventually, his death, confusion and tension rose in the city. Protests began the following week, and the situation changed drastically on the day of Freddie's funeral.

At the time, I was a community school coordinator for an elementary school in the city. Nearly 100 percent of our students were Black, and more than 90 percent were eligible for free and reduced-price meals. Despite the significant challenges that our students and families faced, our school was one of the higher-performing elementary schools in the city, and it was known for its strong community partnerships and ties.

What became most troubling during the period following Freddie Gray's death was the school's proximity to the hot spots of rioting and looting—more positively known as the uprising or unrest. Both the shopping mall and drug store that were featured so prominently on national news after being looted and, in the case of the drug store set on fire, were landmarks on my short commute home.

When word spread about a student-led protest at the mall on the day of the funeral, the anxiety at our school was palpable. We needed to ensure that our students and families were able to get home safely. We did what we could to contact families and make sure that dismissal was smooth and timely.

My fears heightened on my drive home that day when, on my detour to avoid my normal route past the mall, I passed the National Guard and armed tanks filling the street just minutes from my home. I compulsively watched the news that night, seeing familiar places burn, people get injured, and businesses be damaged and robbed. I woke the next morning to find that buildings across the street from my apartment had suffered the same fate.

The next day, due to the growing unrest, school was canceled. Part of me wanted nothing but to leave the city and go somewhere that felt safer. I was apprehensive, but later thankful, when my principal contacted me and said that he was going to open the recreation center attached to our school for students to have a safe place to go for the day. I drove to the school to help him lead the effort.

Our school was fortunate to have committed and engaged community partnerships, and like so many people in Baltimore that day, our partners felt a call to give back and support the communities whose daily and historical struggles were being brought to the fore. Thanks to our partners, the students who came to the center that day got to participate in interactive STEM activities, play sports, and eat a free meal and snacks. While what was happening outside the center walls was scary and uncertain, inside we were able to provide a fun and safe experience for our kids.

Although it was an overwhelmingly positive experience for staff and students, the day was not without challenges. Most of these arose while attempting to manage the outpouring of donations and volunteers that came into our recreation center that day.

People from outside of the neighborhood heard what we were doing and showed up looking for an opportunity to help. However, we were well staffed for the number of students who came, and because we could not legally or ethically have unverified strangers around our children, we ended up having to turn away volunteers.

The day has always been memorable to me as a time when a community came together under a principal who was skilled in leveraging partners for children and families. I have fond memories of sitting with our kids as they excitedly learned about circuits and coding instead of having to worry about what was happening in our city.

When we returned to school the next day, every classroom—no matter the grade level—had an open conversation about the events of the past few days. I truly admired the courage that the teachers demonstrated in having these difficult conversations with young children, helping them make sense of a situation that I myself could not fully comprehend.

Spring 2015 is a time that I will always remember, not only because of how scary it was but also to see how people could come together in a city-wide crisis to support children and families. It is a reminder that leadership is messy and not without flaws but also that when leveraged for good, connections and tough calls can make a tremendously positive impact.

28. Biting

Told by the former director of an urban early childhood center and preschool

During my years as an early childhood center and preschool director, it was *biting* that led to my most significant leadership challenges. Biting is not at all uncommon before the age of 3, occurring most often during the mobile infant and toddler years. Some young children will move through a short phase, whereas more rarely, others will form a biting habit that may take additional support to unlearn. Teething, overstimulation, exhaustion, hunger, and emotional distress can all lead to biting. It's not fun, it hurts, and it's certainly behavior that needs to be addressed, just as throwing or grabbing toys, limit testing, and temper tantrums require intervention.

Unlike other undesirable behaviors seen before, during, and after the terrible 2s, biting can lead to a full-on crisis. It is deeply misunderstood and often viewed as taboo and unforgivable behavior. Within families, siblings and cousins who bite are often stigmatized, and blame is cast on the skills of parents or caregivers. Pediatricians and child psychologists have repeatedly urged parents to not use tactics such as biting back to punish children nor to panic if a child is bitten. It is not a medical emergency, and infection is extremely rare.

Biting plays a role in a larger crisis. Many preschools adopt strict "three strikes and out" policies. The Foundation for Child Development finds that expulsions in preschools are more than three times higher than expulsions from K–12 schools. Boys are expelled at a rate more than four-and-a-half times that of girls. And African American children are twice as likely to be expelled as Latino and white children. African American children are five times more likely to be expelled as Asian American children.[77] These expulsions jeopardize access to important learning and socialization opportunities that promote success in elementary school and beyond. Many preschool expulsions are in response to what are considered "unruly" behaviors, sometimes defined through a lens of racial and cultural bias. And among the unruly behaviors associated with expulsion is biting.

Biting remains emotionally triggering despite evidence about it. A quick internet search points up references to vampires, bad dogs, shark attacks, and cannibalism. Biting was such a big deal that I was asked a question about it during my interview for my job as a preschool director! I have to admit that I took a low-key attitude toward biting, given the science and my own decade-plus experiences around kids who may have bitten now and then as toddlers. Never once did any turn out to be career criminals. I did, however, get serious and draw the line about our response policy at the school.

At my early childhood center and preschool, we ran a developmental program guided by the psychology of early childhood. Under no circumstance would we use suspensions or expulsions to punish biting or any other developmentally related behaviors. Our policy was to teach children the skills they needed to succeed, adjusting the environment and our own practices accordingly. We offered patience and guidance when time was necessary to allow for further brain development.

Our policy worked well, right up until the "patience" part. Every time a biting incident occurred, our staff would document and report to the families involved what happened and what we did in response. When we'd see a hot spot—a class that was seeing a streak of incidents caused by one or more children—we'd communicate openly with all parents about our approach while carefully keeping the students anonymous. Parents of infants and 1-year-olds were mine. I had brought these parents into the school and had started classes on childhood development that prepared them for biting. We had formed parent-to-parent connections and encouraged families to socialize together. We had built strong communities that were resilient when biting episodes occurred. These parents understood the process and trusted the school's expertise and response plan.

However, the parents of our 2-year-olds had been brought in by my predecessor. They did not experience the same bonding and education in their years at the school. They remained tired and bitter about biting that had happened when their babies were younger. From their perspective, something was going wrong when they had

---

[77] Child Welfare League of America (2020).

to deal with biting year after year, and they felt that they could never get a break from worrying their child might come home with a distinct bite mark and bruise. These parents didn't want a solution that would work in a month or two. They wanted the biting to stop *now*. The best way to ensure the biting stopped instantly, in their eyes, was to exclude the biter(s) from the school. Frequent and open communication and sharing data on biting incidents should have reduced their concerns and anxiety, but it backfired. To them, the school was accepting biting behavior and protecting the "bad" children. These parents were not willing to wait for the school's interventions to work.

We brought in a child psychologist to observe and advise the classroom teachers on their interventions and even had a pediatrician hold a meeting with parents to address their concerns. Coming after the biting had happened, parents simply weren't as open and receptive, and it did little to assuage their fears. It's important to note that the parents of young children can be emotionally vulnerable. They are often sleep deprived, stressed, and worried. At times they feel guilty about leaving their children in school. In these situations, the psychological extent of the threat and the precariousness of our ties as a community were revealed. The social compact with these families felt broken. A flash point came with a mom yelling at one of my teachers inside the classroom in front of the children—a full breakdown of trust on both sides. In the end, we asked that family to leave the school, and several other families chose to withdraw their children too. It was a tough and sad time.

Since then, I've thought a lot about the way schools consider the emotional needs of families and how we were able to form a more nurturing community by providing education and social support for our newer families. Proactively learning the science behind toddler behavior helps families prepare themselves for tough times. It helps them not view other parents or the school to be at fault. We were able to confront the cultural taboo and social shame that biting can exacerbate. I wonder that if our 2-year-old classroom parents had had access to the same supports, things would have played out differently for them. For me, it was a lesson in what it takes to build strong caring relationships with families, to be compassionate toward them even in the face of what seems like unjust and unmerited intolerance, and to remain committed to loving and teaching our children all the more when they need us the most.

29. The Magnolia

Told by an administrator of the Recovery School District

I was helping a steering committee, The Friends of L. B. Landry, redesign L. B. Landry High School in the Algiers community in New Orleans. The committee was led by Pastor Arthur Wardsworth from 2nd Good Hope Baptist Church. L. B. Landry first opened to serve this community as an elementary school in 1938 and converted to a high school in 1942. It would be the first high school rebuilt after Hurricane Katrina.

Algiers was the only part of New Orleans proper across the river. You could get there by crossing the bridge or taking the Canal Street Ferry straight to Algiers Point. Because of its isolated location across the river, and because it was the "Black" community, Algiers was historically last on the minds of most New Orleans politicians and business community.

When Landry High School was destroyed, not so much by the storm as by FEMA using it as headquarters, the community was left without its beloved school. Students had to go across the river or had to attend a charter school hastily opened after the storm on the other side of Algiers. When it was time to do some rebuilding, L. B. Landry was not on the "immediate" list. It was the dedicated community groups that stood up and demanded that they not be last in line anymore that led to L. B. Landry being selected for rebuilding.

After the Friends of L. B. Landry earned the right to have their school rebuilt, I was asked by the Recovery School District (RSD) to sit on the steering committee and be a liaison among the school community, school partners, RSD, and the builders. I was tasked with building partnerships, gathering input on academic design, and even having some input into the physical design of the new school. I was reminded early and often by Pastor Wardsworth that Landry was to be a community school based on community needs.

The best part of this experience was witnessing the love that community members had for this school, this community, and each other. It wasn't just a building and a set of programs they were rebuilding. They were rebuilding the institution that so many saw as central to the identity of their community. The Algiers community had gone through so much before, during, and after Katrina. This was a special time for them to get back the cornerstone of the community.

We held monthly steering committee meetings to plan the redesign. Before and after each meeting, we held meetings at 2nd Good Hope Church to seek input and have open dialogue about the design with members of the larger community. We had so much great input. There were heated arguments occasionally, but everyone shared a common wish to build something special.

Most community members were thrilled by the sheer scope and quality of design mock-ups of the new building, the Health Sciences Hub, the Process Technology Hub, and the fully functioning Community Health Center being added by Tulane University. The community was excited about getting its school back in a new and improved form.

However, conversations kept coming back to the lonely magnolia tree that stood tall outside the old building that was about to be taken down. It had been around forever, surviving multiple hurricanes prior to Katrina. It had even survived FEMA when the building did not. When we talked about the location of the new space, community members would ask questions like, "Will that be where the tree is?" Digging deeper, people started telling me stories of how they met their friends by the tree before and after school, how they would sit under the shade of the tree during hot days, how they stole their first kiss from the kids who ended up to becoming their spouses of 10, 20, 30, and 40 years.

After several community meetings and steering committee meetings, we went to the architects and RSD and told them that we had to build this school around that magnolia tree. That tree meant too much to everyone here, and we couldn't see having the one without the other. A good amount of money was spent keeping that tree healthy during construction, and in the end the school was built in a horseshoe shape around that magnolia tree.

The school had no principal during this time. However, the woman who was eventually chosen to be the principal was a former staff member of the school and a member of the community who regularly attended our meetings. Indeed, she was a central force in leading the steering committee to recommend building the school around the tree.

30. No One Saw It Coming

Told by the head of the middle school of an urban K–12 independent school

I stared at the clock as I listened on the phone in disbelief. It was 10:21 p.m. on a Wednesday night. I remember the details of that evening vividly despite the many years that have passed.

I was in my second year as head of the Middle School, still awake that night after speaking to my wife who was in Dallas with our 1-year-old daughter for a family visit.

The call came from Jenny, assistant head of the Middle School. She was emotional, and it was difficult to comprehend what she was telling me. She was at the home of our sixth-grade science teacher, Ann, who had found her 10-year-old son hanging from a belt in his closet. He was dead.

Peter had been a fifth grader at our school, a perfectly healthy, well-developing child, although somewhat quiet. He was fond of the outdoors, like his mother, and loved riding his bike. There was no reason to think that he was suicidal and no explanation for why he would have taken his own life. No one saw it coming.

As I laid awake most of the night, infinite questions raced through my mind: Who else knows? Who would Ann want me to tell? What would she want me to say? How much should they hear about the actual cause of death? Should I be the one to tell her teaching team and other colleagues? Who's going to cover her classes? What should we tell her students about why she's going to be out for the foreseeable future? How long should I encourage her to take off from school? What about Peter's classmates and teachers? Should parents hear from us before their children do, so they can help their children cope? What resources should we be providing for parents, students, and colleagues? What did Ann need from me? Did she even know I knew? What should we be doing for her sixth-grade daughter, Rita, who lost her brother so tragically? How would the family cope? Ann was a single parent, having lost her husband, Peter and Rita's father, to cancer several years before.

The next 72 hours were filled with a flurry of the most difficult conversations I've ever had, a heaviness inside that left me sad and nauseous, nonstop meetings with colleagues and mental health professionals, and little sleep. Early the next morning and with the help of many, we developed a strategy about how we would share the news of Peter's death. Email was not a viable option, even for reaching parents. Those many years ago, only some of our families had internet access at home, and fewer still had email accounts.

We needed a plan that would control the spread of information and limit rumors and that would provide enough information to avoid creating mystery around Peter's death while at the same time sharing the truth in a gentle enough way to also avoid reactions of panic and fear. We wanted to arm the adults at school and at home with the language and resources to address each child's reaction to the stunning news and to know how best to support them in the days following—all that after coping with their own reactions.

I decided that Thursday would be the day we share the news with adults, working inside out. First, I'd talk to other administrators in the school, then to those on Ann's sixth-grade teaching team, and to Peter's fifth-grade teachers. I tried to do this late enough in the day so that the teachers, knowing they'd be shaken, would be more likely to feel they could stay and finish the day.

Naturally, word of the tragedy spread quickly within the Middle School, and we announced an urgent K–12 faculty meeting for that afternoon, taking place in the band room. We never had faculty meetings in the band room—it was located in a remote corner of campus. There was an ominous feeling among faculty and staff as we made our way there after dismissal.

We had an interim head of school that year, and because she didn't know Peter or Ann well—nor the details of Peter's death and his family that I did—she turned it over to me from the start. I remember feeling so tired and nervous as I stood in front of this huge group for the first time. I could see on their faces who had heard the news already and who had not. Those who hadn't were visibly worried.

I told the story from the beginning, describing Jenny's phone call the night before, and shared the few details I knew up to that point. I read aloud the parent letter I had written earlier in the day between meetings, that we had frantically distributed to all Middle School students moments before at dismissal time, along with an article on coping with grief, asking students to make sure their parents read it when they arrived home.

Lower School teachers knew Peter, and everyone knew Ann, a beloved and highly respected colleague. The heaviness and sadness in that band room is hard to describe. I've never felt a group of people ache together so deeply. Some cried. Most sat quietly in disbelief, worried about Ann and Rita. Eventually a few questions surfaced, and I shared our plans to have mental health professionals available at school for days to come. People wanted to help. Ann's science department colleagues offered to help plan lessons and cover classes. Initial plans to provide food for the family took shape. Others volunteered to organize a collection to help with funeral and other costs. There was so much to do and still so much we didn't know.

The faculty meeting was followed by a meeting of mental health professionals from around the city who had responded to our call for help. It was a who's who of the top doctors in town, and they all looked to me to put them to work. But I didn't know what we needed. I was having trouble thinking clearly. We hadn't even told the students yet of Peter's death, so I didn't know what the needs would be for supporting them. I shared with the counselors what I knew up to that point and what I was planning for the next day, and then they helped construct a support plan for students and faculty. It was far-reaching: all high schoolers who spent their sixth-grade year at our school had had Ann as their science teacher, and they loved her. They would be rocked and would need help, too.

Joe was one of the counselors I leaned on that day. He invited me back to his house after the meeting and ordered some food. With my family still out of town, I had no one to go home to, and I needed some quiet time with someone who understood. That Thursday had been the longest day of my life.

Friday morning began with an assembly for all of the Middle School. Teachers knew what was coming, but few students did. I had rehearsed my words the night before at Joe's, but that didn't curb my nervousness. I thought I might vomit, and I remember walking outside for some air as the kids piled into the multipurpose room. Faculty, administrators, a few parents, and several counselors stood around the room as I began speaking.

I recall telling students of Peter's death, that we thought it was an accident (which was true), and that each of us reacts differently to tragic situations like this based on who we are and our own life experiences. I explained there is no one way to react, no certain way you're supposed to feel. Anything is justified. What's most important is to have the courage to talk about it with an adult you trust.

As I spoke, students looked around the room at each other as middle schoolers do, trying to echo-locate to determine what their own reaction should be. Older girls cried. Rebecca, a seventh grader, sat right in front of me, and I watched as her eyes welled up and she fought hard not to cry out loud. I remember how much I hated the fact that I was the one causing so much pain for these children. I was the one telling this awful story that would make them feel so sad and scared, a story they would never forget.

As the room emptied, I walked down the hallway and into the Middle School office. A few colleagues were in there and a few lingering parents. No one wanted to leave, but no one knew what to do. Something was said that made me start to cry, and my administrative assistant got up and told me to sit in her chair. I did, and I proceeded to cry with my head in my hands. It might have been 10 minutes—I lost all track of time. It was the first time I had cried since Peter died, and I couldn't stop. I remember several people rubbing my back and saying kind things, but mostly it was quiet in the office except for my sobbing.

School went on that day, but it was surreal. We had decided routine was important, but so was the chance for kids to decide for themselves if they needed something different. Several students visited counselors that day. Many parents picked up their kids early.

The funeral home held visiting hours Saturday afternoon. The room was packed. I talked quietly with colleagues who had the same sick feeling in their stomachs as I did. Eventually I got to the front of the line and encountered Ann for the first time since her son's death. We embraced, and she whispered in my ear, "Thank you for everything." And I, fighting back tears, whispered back, "I wish I could do more." I looked over her shoulder at the smallest coffin I've ever seen and then left the building, wiping away tears and thinking of my 1-year old daughter.

My life will be forever linked to the people with whom I lived through the tragedy of Peter's death, none more than Ann. Every year on October 20 for the past 20 years, I write her a note. I want her to know that I still remember her beautiful boy and that he will never be forgotten. He touched many lives in his short time on earth, and I feel lucky to have known him. As a parent myself, that's what I would want to hear from people who knew my child.

In the first few years after Peter died, I encouraged Ann to take the day off on the anniversary of his death. Sometimes she did but mostly not. It has to be hard beyond words for Ann when the anniversary of her son's death cycles around. How do you simultaneously hold onto the love and memory of your child when it is accompanied with unspeakable pain and loss? I want Ann to know that she is never alone in her pain, that I still remember what happened so long ago.

Ann still works at my school, and she still teaches sixth-grade science. She is the longest-tenured faculty member in our Middle School, a testament to her talent as an educator, to her courage, and to the strength and support she must have felt from our school community over many years.

I learned so much about life, leadership, and caretaking from the people and circumstances surrounding Peter's death. I think often about Peter and wonder what he'd be doing if he were alive now. He would be the same age today as I was at the time this story unfolded.

31. No Hugs, No Bugs

Told by the principal of an urban public elementary school

It was hardly fathomable that anything could shut down America's schools. In my city, we've had blizzards and arctic blasts that have closed them, but these events have been localized and never lasted long. As news of a strange virus began to circulate, it didn't occur to me that what was going on so far away would be part of our lives and so dramatically affect our small elementary school. For in fact, it is "our" school—ours in the sense of the community we have built within the school among students, teachers, staff, and parents and ours in the sense that this school belongs to the community and the families we serve.

Our school had recently received a technology modernization grant that allowed us to provide technology for each student and teacher. It was part of an effort by the school district to help close the gap between the haves and the have-nots. When news broke that the number of states with growing numbers of coronavirus cases was increasing, I knew I had to figure out how to swiftly get our new learning devices from our classrooms and into the hands of students if we were to have to shelter like what was being reported elsewhere.

What I knew to be true was that my students would need laptops to continue to learn at home with the many online learning platforms that we had at school. Despite safety concerns and prior to any district plan for distribution, I set up a system for students and parents to pick up their devices from school. It was good that we acted quickly. Soon the district would close all its schools and keep them closed for an unprecedented amount of time.

Although we were closed for in-person learning, my work as principal continued. The district considered building administrators "essential workers." It relied on us to lead our schools in remote learning. It relied on us to ensure that meals would be distributed to children eligible for them. There was a great deal of other work we were expected to do, much of it inside the school building. My concerns for reporting to school grew into anxiety as I worried whether leaving home would place my family—my husband, my children, and my immune-sensitive 79-year-old mother—at risk of getting sick. The stress became intense, and I began to doubt. I didn't want to worry about my school community anymore. I didn't want to report to work anymore and risk contracting COVID. I wished for the impossible—a bubble around my home so that my family and I could hunker down until the pandemic passed.

That was until my internal spiritual compass pointed me in a new direction. "If not you, then who? If not now, when?" It became important to me that I get smart, wade through the CDC's and state's health guidelines, and make both my home and my school community as safe as possible. I began to think about how to make my school a healthy place for students and teachers to return in the fall, thinking that by then, surely the virus curve will have flattened, allowing us to reopen for in-person learning.

Thinking about reopening at the beginning of the upcoming school year meant messaging to the school community what a return to school would look like. I thought about creating a brochure, sending video messages on social media, and hosting virtual community meetings. In my adult mind, all of these things sounded like viable options to inform parents and children about what to expect.

Then one of my energetic, sometimes nonconforming, kindergarteners, Xavier, reminded me that I also had to think about this as a child

approaching the return to school. It had been several months since our students were abruptly torn from their home away from home and since they were disconnected from their classmates and the adults who cared about them. From my office window, I could see Xavier and his mom walking to school to pick up a kindergarten learning packet and several to-go meals. I hurried to the main entrance door and held it open for them, so happy to see a student's face.

The fall and winter of his first year in a school—before COVID—had been quite an adjustment for Xavier. He and I spent a lot of time together redirecting his behavior after he caused interruptions in his classroom. I discovered that Xavier had a love and talent for singing gospel songs. I helped him become the youngest member of our school choir so that he could have an outlet to channel his energies doing something he loved and to help him focus his attention when he returned to the classroom. Xavier knew, and the staff knew, that he had become one of my special students whom I had taken under my wing. Every time Xavier would see me in the building, he would run to embrace me with a hug.

As Xavier and his mother turned the corner and headed up the walkway to the school entrance, he saw me. "Ms. Greene!" He yanked his hand away from his mother's to run into my arms. His mother couldn't catch him. As he was running toward me, I was thinking that at the moment he had no idea about social distancing and that hugging me was off limits. In a split second, I had to make the difficult decision to ward off his embrace. When I held out my hands to stop him, his face contorted into confusion. I instinctively knew that I should have hugged him and hoped that all would be well. Xavier's mother and I tried to explain to him why we couldn't embrace, but his face told it all. His principal with whom he had a special relationship had rejected him.

There had to be a better way to lead a return-to-school campaign. I needed to figure out something that would help students understand that although we would have to do things differently to stay safe from the virus, our school was still the same warm, welcoming, loving place. I needed to figure out how to communicate that although we would need to wear masks, practice social distancing, and take other health precautions that might feel strange, uncomfortable, and alienating, we were still the same school where, pre-COVID, we would fist bump, hug, and dance to the Electric Slide, Wobble, and Cupid Shuffle to start our morning classes. I would have to figure out different routines for the start of the school day that would allow me and my morning operations team to get close to our kids and gauge what side of bed they got up on and to figure

out which students had endured a rough night because of violence in the home or scarcity of food.

It was then that *No Hugs. No Bugs.* was born. I created and published a children's storybook of puppy characters who were navigating their return to school during COVID. The pups showed students about getting temperatures taken at the door, greeting and interacting with each other safely, washing their hands, and keeping six feet apart. Students would see that even though we were taking steps to stay safe and healthy, our school could still be a place where caring and empathy lie at the heart of our home away from home.

Mask Up—Julia D'Agostino, PreK

---

32. Two Storms in One Week

Told by the chief administrator of a small-town charter school

We are a public charter school serving 750 students in fifth through 12th grades. We are located in a small southeastern town near the Atlantic coast, and our students reside in nine surrounding rural, low-income counties. Our mission is to inspire and prepare students with STEM-related skills, knowledge, and attitudes needed to meet future challenges in the global workforce and their communities.

After our first year of operation in a temporary facility on a university campus, we were provided

a larger space capable of supporting our growing enrollment. The move was a grand affair welcomed by students, parents, staff, and our board. As the new school year approached, our full school community came out with smiling faces and able bodies to spruce up the facility and make it our own. School spirit filled the air. Our new facility offered a sense of permanence and belonging to our stakeholders, who having taken a true leap of faith to be a part of our school's creation and could finally breathe a sigh of relief in knowing that the school now had a forever home.

Or so we thought.

Just 6 weeks into the new school year, our region faced a tropical storm system that wreaked havoc in our community. The hurricane caused many areas to flood, and we experienced the typical aftermath: trees down, roof damage, power outages. Of course, the nicely manicured landscaping everyone had worked so hard to complete was dislodged or destroyed completely. The freshly painted rooms and students' artwork were damaged from roof leaks. And our auditorium suffered major damage to the stage and seating areas. To top it all off, the HVAC system did not recover from the outage, leaving warm, moist air to linger throughout the facility.

And then the second storm system arrived.

Within a week of the first storm, another major tropical system pounded the region. Our ecosystem simply could not absorb the water and winds from this second storm, nor could our facility. When we returned to our building after this second wave of weather, we were devastated by what we found. Mold. Lots of mold. Mold on walls, mold on furniture, mold in classroom plants and student work samples. Mold everywhere. The facility was uninhabitable.

With no facility in which to operate, our very existence was at stake. Our public charter school is not a member of any charter school network to fall back on. There was no central office or school district to provide a security blanket. And there were no other buildings capable of housing our school in the entire region that did not need substantial renovations. I'll never, ever forget the sleepless nights and weeklong days, running over in my mind how I would explain to our students and parents, to my colleagues and friends, to our founding board members who had sacrificed so much, to the organizations that had placed their trust in us—*to the entire region*—that I had failed them and that our school was forced to close. In an instant, there was intense crisis.

As the school's founding leader, all eyes were pointed directly at me, and I remember feeling so ill prepared for such a daunting challenge. Nobody ever teaches you how to manage a crisis like this in your educational leadership courses or in any professional development workshops. I dare say you will find few, if any, Major Crises 101 or Save Your School 211 courses in the nearest university catalog. Immediately, "What's the plan?" emails and phone calls flooded in from all around. I distinctly recall one parent's plea, which was representative of so many: "My child has never felt like he belonged until your school came along. If this school closes, I don't know what we'll do." And staff, "Will I have a job next week? What do I tell my children? We live paycheck to paycheck, and I can't not have a job."

As soon as we realized the extent of the damages and their initial implications, the board and I took action. We held difficult conversations with university representatives regarding how we might return to the temporary facility on their campus. After intensive efforts, we devised a plan to temporarily occupy different vacant spaces throughout the campus. On Thursdays, we met to review a list of spaces that were scheduled to be vacant on specific days and times the following two weeks and selected those that would house our students—*our school*. On Friday afternoons, we moved necessary resources to these locations for the following week and notified students and parents. Students and staff quickly learned how to navigate the university campus to say the least!

We purchased rolling carts so that teachers could better traverse the campus with their classroom supplies. When students and staff said that they felt disconnected, we scheduled grade-level and schoolwide events that could be held outside during the regular school day. On days when sufficient space wasn't available on campus, we collaborated with organizations across the region to hold "remote learning days" that featured our teachers collaborating with community organizations to facilitate hands-on learning for students. From these activities, we developed a full ecosystem to support remote learning—tech tools, training, policies and procedures, an instructional framework, and so on—that, as serendipity would have it, served our school quite well years later during the global COVID pandemic.

Looking back on this crisis, I can say with complete conviction that it was only by demonstrating principles of committed and caring leadership that we navigated through the uncertainty to realize tremendous successes in the years afterward. I took time to talk with students and treated them as equals. I reassured them that we would persevere through our temporary challenges, and I carefully engaged them in solving pieces of the larger problems we faced so that they felt like compatriots in the work. I called parents to learn more about what they were experiencing so that we could better meet the needs of our school family.

At our full staff meetings, no question was off limits. I frequently met with students and parents, and I offered unwavering assurance that our team would not rest until we had successfully overcome this latest challenge in our school's short history. When local media peppered me and the board with questions each week, we responded with confidence that our team was extremely creative, dedicated to our vision of becoming a model for next-generation teaching and learning, and tackling the challenges of the day in stride. We took what little time we had to celebrate our successes, no matter how small.

When progress report and report card times came, I wrote a personal note on each one, for every student, without exception. Each and every day, I made it a habit to handwrite and place in the mail at least one personal note to a staff member, parent, or student. I traveled from class to class across the campus to talk with students and staff about our work, about their interests. I played cards with students in the university cafeteria and kicked soccer balls with them at recess. I made voice recordings as I walked across the campus and on the long rides home and emailed them to students and staff to thank them for their tenacity. Years later, on many occasions, parents, students, and staff alike have shared with me that the notes and the time I devoted to getting to know them made all the difference in building trust and maintaining their allegiance to our school as we overcame the crisis—together.

Tornado—Sebastian Hetrick, Grade 5

33. And Then There Was Mold

Told by the principal of a suburban public elementary school

Over the course of three school years, I had gone from what felt like a brand-new and energized principal to a weathered and beaten-down veteran. The fall of the first year brought 9/11, which I thought would be the height of all the "bad stuff" that was a part of being a school administrator. Fast-forward to the next fall, and I found myself at a Board of Education meeting to discuss closing our school because of mold.

When I first arrived as my school's new principal, I was told during a walkthrough with the current director of Buildings and Grounds of an "old issue" of mold in the building. I would come to find out later that there was indeed a serious problem.

The cleanliness and air quality of the building were always one of my top priorities. As I got to know the staff better, I learned that one of the teachers had been complaining of health-related issues for several years, issues that she attributed to the air quality in the building. It was at that time that I brought this to the attention of district administration. I was told that there was once a "very small issue" that had been mitigated, and there was nothing I should be concerned about. I took comfort in believing that the issue had been addressed. Yet I continued being vigilant about the cleanliness of the building.

I was excited to begin my third year as principal of my school. I had developed some wonderful relationships with the parents and families of the school community. A few weeks into the school year, one of our student's moms called me on the phone. There was a lot of concern in her voice as she explained that her daughter was coming home from school every day and having severe nosebleeds. She went on to say that any time outside of school her daughter was completely fine. Yet on school days, she experienced these nosebleeds when she got home. I contacted our school nurse, who then contacted the parents and discussed their child's health issue. Having some knowledge of the history of the building, I reached out to district administration to inform them of my conversation with the mother and to ask for guidance. I was told to monitor the situation and if any changes happened to let them know.

Over the next several weeks, the school nurse and I stayed in daily contact with the parents. We also had the child's classroom teacher monitoring the situation as well. As the days went by, the student continued to experience all of the health-related concerns that her parents told us about. I began to take her out of her classroom twice daily to walk, get some fresh air, and get a drink of water. This continued for approximately 2 weeks, and we seemed to be making some progress. This accommodation that the classroom teacher permitted, along with the other accommodations we provided, seemed to make things a little better.

A few weeks later I received a phone call from district administration telling me that it was not necessary for me to be speaking with the parent on a daily basis, and there was no need for me to be walking with the student around the building. I was instructed that all further communication with this parent, with regard to the child's health, would come from district administration. I reached out to the parents to tell them what I was told to do and that moving forward they would communicate about this matter with district administration. Within a few days, the student transferred to a different elementary school in the district.

Early in the morning that Saturday, my phone rang. It was the superintendent calling to tell me that the Board of Education would be closing my building the following Tuesday. I was informed that all of the students in my building were going to be split up and transferred to the four other elementary schools in the district. Our secretary, our nurse, and I would be joining the kindergarten through second-grade teachers and students in the building that also housed our central office personnel. I was instructed to complete an itinerant schedule for all of the students and all of the other buildings and to reach out to the principals of these other schools to discuss where our students' classes would be. The only information I was given about my school was that the district was going to have an environmental analysis conducted. Throughout the entire process, I was excluded from all discussions. I was only notified of the decisions that were made and what I needed to do to implement them.

More than 300 parents flooded the Board of Education's meeting that month to discuss the closing of our school. The board had established a special committee made up of board members, parents, faculty, and staff and charged it to deal with the mold problem at our school and at any other school in the district. Many parents addressed board members in loud voices, spoke out of turn, and angrily told them about health issues their children had struggled with while attending our school. Some health issues went back years. The parent who initially brought her daughter's health concerns to my attention stated that her daughter had suffered from chronic nosebleeds, headaches, and severe congestion. Another parent stood and asked parents to raise their hands if they thought any of their children had suffered nosebleeds, headaches, congestion, sinus problems, or asthma. About 30 parents raised their hands, indicating that their children had displayed similar symptoms. It was at this point that the district administration said that it was unaware of any health-related issues at the school until they were contacted by the students' parents.

Over the course of the next 5 months I went to my now closed school every day to oversee the arrival of our students, load them on a bus to be transported to their temporary school, and then headed to my temporary desk to begin my day. For every one of those days I would visit all of our students at the four other elementary schools to check in, making sure they were being supported. I also wanted to make sure that they all knew we were all going to be back together soon.

I was continuously left out of discussions on the remediation plan for our school building as well as any timeline of return. After many months of testing, samples showed evidence of mold in the carpet in the library and the faculty room. There was visible mold in a classroom ceiling closet and in six other classrooms. After remediation was completed, we were scheduled to return to our building in mid-spring. The reopening ended a 5-month ordeal.

Soon after our return, I was meeting district administration for my annual evaluation. I was told at that meeting that I was not going to be recommended for renewal. The reason I was given was that they did not see me developing into the instructional leader that was in the best interest of the district.

I believe that everything that we do in school leadership is to be a champion for the kids. If you make all of your decisions in the best interest of kids, you will never make a bad decision. Now, almost 20 years later and in a different school district, I continue to live by this ideal. I am not going to allow students to ever have an experience with me that isn't anything other than positive and uplifting! It took a while to move past the mold crisis in my school and the way the district handled it. But if I learned anything, it is that if you ever need to be reminded of why you do what you do, sit back and watch the incredible resilience of children.

34. I Am Here for You

Told by an associate director of an independent high school

A few years ago, independent schools, along with far too many other institutions and industries across the country, were grappling with a series of stories, allegations, and investigations regarding historical, ongoing or sometimes systemic sexual assault and abuse. The *Boston Globe*'s investigative team, Spotlight, and their Pulitzer Prize–winning exposé of sexual abuse by Catholic priests was receiving another wave of recognition, and more attention was being devoted to issues of sexual abuse due to the release and commercial success of the 2015 Academy Award–winning film by the same name. A year later in 2016, the *Boston Globe* team of reporters published a report highlighting widespread sexual abuse in some of the nation's most historic and elite private schools. More specifically that year and in following years, a number of boarding schools, some of which are highly regarded as the best in the country, would also find themselves embroiled in cases of sexual misconduct.

The world of independent schools is relatively small; the community of boarding schools is even smaller and more interconnected. Due to the familiarity of and collegiality among our schools, the faculty and staff of my school viewed these stories through a personal lens, and we found it especially upsetting and alarming that atrocities like this could have occurred in settings and among communities so similar to our own. Simultaneously though, as stories arose and abuse was uncovered at other schools, there was an increasing sense of relief that we were not among the schools involved in any scandal and a growing confidence that our school was not capable of such misconduct—or so we thought.

We were forced to face a much different reality when, in the summer of 2016, a report of historic sexual abuse by a retired and widely beloved teacher at our school was shared with our new head of school, Kristin Taylor. To provide some context, this was Kristin's first time in the role as a head of school. She had worked at a number of other independent schools throughout her career, and most recently, she had served as the dean of students at another boarding school. In our institution's long history, she is only the seventh head to be named, and she is the first woman to serve in this capacity. Furthermore, she had only set foot on campus twice during the interview and selection process, and she was still in the process of moving her family to campus and getting to know the community and school when these allegations came to light in early summer. She was still in her first few months at our school when she was forced to confront a difficult past and to lead an entire school community in reconciling with some difficult truths.

Kristin's handling of the sexual abuse at our school remains one of the most poignant examples of care I've witnessed. The allegations were immediately reported to the appropriate authorities and, in addition to an investigation by law enforcement, she hired an independent firm to conduct its own investigation to uncover the full extent of abuse and report it to appropriate authorities. Alumni were contacted and encouraged to come forward to the police or the investigators to share additional reports, and a number of other actions and steps were taken that went beyond what is legally required of any institution in this situation.

I don't downplay the importance of the legal steps she took, but they are less critical in conveying the depth of care she exemplified in the coming weeks and months. Early in the process, Kristin gathered the entire faculty and staff to share news of the abuse. She outlined the process moving forward and briefed us on what information was available. After sharing the logistics of the investigations, she spoke to us personally, unscripted, and in tears:

> I know how incredibly hard it is to hear this news, and I cannot begin to understand the various emotions this may evoke. You may be distraught, confused, in disbelief, angry, hurt, or saddened. I assure you that whatever you are feeling is OK. There is no right way to feel. This will affect us each in different ways. I want you to know that your emotions are valid, they are real, and they are acceptable—do not ignore them and do not bury them. What we need to do now is to lean on each other, speak with each other, and to come together for support. I do not have all the answers, and I cannot promise perfection. I can promise to do the right thing. I, and we as a school, will do everything we can to support and protect the individuals who were harmed, and I will do all I can to ensure the well-being of our employees and the safety and health of our students. I will be transparent, honest, and forthright, and I am here to support you.

Days later, Kristin contacted all students, parents, and members of the school community with the information learned thus far and to ensure her support for anyone in need. External counselors were made available for anyone struggling with the news. She personally held open individual and group meetings for anyone needing support or were interested in speaking further.

In the following weeks, Kristin seemed to be everywhere at all times, checking in on faculty, dropping by offices and classrooms, taking students aside, speaking with parents and community members, and listening to those struggling with the situation. The world today often seems so litigious that it can feel impossible to communicate and act in a truly personal and caring way—not to mention during such a difficult and emotionally complex case of historic sexual abuse. The instinctual reaction of so many people and organizations amid wrongdoing seems to be to say the right words, recede into the background away from the public eye, mitigate any consequences, and then move on. However, Kristin remained transparent, authentic, available, and humble, and she stayed committed to connecting with and supporting members of the school community, even when she didn't know what the solution might be. She did not distance herself from the uncomfortable truths of the past, nor did she shield the school from scrutiny or criticism. She embraced the messiness and complexity of what it means to care for and love something, and through her acts, she set the example and showed us how to come together, confront failures, learn, and grow both as individuals and as a school.

Heart and Hands—Noa Stern Frede, Grade 8

35. Winning and Losing

Told by the principal of an urban public high school

Our city, and in particular the Latino and African American neighborhoods of the students and families we serve, has been struggling for years with poor, untrusting relationships with the police, police shootings, and the excessive use of force by police. Although much of this story takes place outside our community, this context is important to how the events of the story were experienced.

One year before this story takes place, police officers shot and killed an African American teenager. The shooting did not attract widespread attention until a year later—a few months before this story takes place—when footage from police officers' body cameras was released. Large-scale protests broke out across the city. Neighborhoods were roiled. It was only after the video was released that the officer who fired the fatal shots was charged with murder. At the time, no other officer on the scene was charged with any offense. One month later, the state attorney general ordered a civil rights investigation of police tactics in the city. Also that month, the U.S. Department of Justice began an investigation into police shootings and excessive use of force. It would be an understatement to say that community–police relations were strained. For many, these relations were broken.

This story unfolds in the spring of my first year as a principal and my first year as principal of Humboldt High. I am a white female who comes from an upper-middle income professional family. I had turned 30 the year before. Our school enrolled about 3,000 students, about 85 percent of whom were Latino, 12 percent were African American, and less than 2 percent were white. We had large numbers of low-income students and large numbers of students whose first language was not English.

We were riding a winning basketball season and going to the state tournament. We were good, a long-standing powerhouse in the state but ever the underdog. We had only one senior starter on our team. We began the season unranked but earned a berth in the state tournament. We won our early games and found ourselves in the finals as underdogs to more heavily favored teams, both perennial state finalists and champions.

On Thursday night, we played a predominantly white parochial academy in the semifinal game. The game was a nail-biter that we won by two points.

"Ooh, aah, you shoulda been a Raptor! Ooh, aah, you shoulda been a Raptor!" Our students were bursting with deserved excitement and school pride.

Their chants continued to echo in the atrium of the arena as we waited while each of our almost 30 students visited the restroom before boarding the fan bus for the 3-hour ride home. By the time the group was ready, the venue was almost empty. We left through the same doors we entered, but we didn't see the bus. Instead, we saw a wall of fans of the school we had beaten—some teenagers, some adults. There was no security or crowd control, and there was no path forward.

Immediately, objects came flying at us, mostly concession stand items, like cups of soda and hotdogs. Our students stayed back and returned fire with insults and any food they were carrying. At that point, the situation felt bothersome more than anything. But when one of the adults from the other school launched a parking cone toward our students and hit Marcene, a petite sophomore girl, in the face, tensions flared. Insults turned to profanity and three of our students stepped forward and clashed with the other crowd as they moved toward us.

I knew we had to keep the groups separated to prevent an all-out brawl. I, along with three of our security guards who had traveled with us as chaperones, directed our students back into the arena. We were able to get most of our students into the vestibule between two sets of entry doors, where they continued yelling. Once in the vestibule, we became less concerned for their physical safety.

I stepped back outside to calm the handful of our students who remained outside on the sidewalk and to move them inside. One of our security guards and two of our students were attending to Marcene, who was on the ground outside the doors, bleeding profusely from her mouth and having trouble breathing because of her emotions. Many of us were messy—covered in ketchup and cola. But it felt like we had avoided a major incident and we just needed to wait for an escort to take us to our bus.

As if on cue, local police officers began responding to the scene from inside the arena. But we could see in the way they were approaching that they were not coming to assess the situation and assist. They marched toward us in a line formation with their riot batons drawn. They opened the first set of doors to the vestibule and began yelling at us to "disperse." They used their batons in a cross-checking motion to shove our kids outside and back into the crowd.

Chaos ensued. Some of our students were pulled and dragged into the crowd. More police arrived in cars and mobile units with riot gear. They stood around the perimeter, boxing in the two conflicting groups yelling, "Disperse! We will fire pepper bombs! Disperse!" But there was no place for us to go. The police who came from inside the arena fully cleared the vestibule and continued to use their batons to push our kids further onto the street and deeper into the crowd—and into the riot officers.

I felt like I had no way to guide our students to safety. Some huddled in corners away from the conflict. Others formed a physical barrier to protect Marcene. Still others were in physical conflict with the opposing fans. I was certain there were some students I couldn't see. I approached an officer who seemed to be commanding the others and asked with panic, "Where should I send them? Where should I send my students for safety? We have nowhere to go!" He did not respond but continued to robotically repeat his orders to disperse. Then he used his baton to shove me strongly back into the crowd.

Our students began yelling to each other, "We have to get out of here!" They knew we had to find our own way out. And they began to run away from the arena and found the bus around the corner. Our security guards began directing students toward the bus. Simultaneously, I saw a senior student of ours, Carlos, being tackled to the ground by a police officer. After he was face-down on the cement, a second officer jumped on top of him. Carlos's best friend, Estéban, was nearby and was clubbed in the back of the head with a baton.

As we arrived at our bus, our school security officers tried to calm our students and check them for injuries. I requested an ambulance for Marcene. Carlos was handcuffed and put in the back of a police car for "aggravated assault of an officer." Estéban had run to the bus, but we escorted him to a first-aid station after he complained of light-headedness. The first-aid station called an ambulance to have him checked for a concussion.

There I was, a first-year principal, minutes after our semifinal victory, standing in the middle of a street in a different town looking at two students in ambulances, one in the back of a police car, and a bus full of students and staff who had been assailed by an angry crowd and then by police officers. I thought of the families, the students, the colleagues, and the district officials who trusted me to ensure everyone's safety. I wondered if anyone would believe what we experienced. I toggled between anger and disbelief for the lack of organization and security at the arena and for the escalating and volatile response from the police. I wanted an explanation. I wanted to see security video footage. Foremost, I wanted to take care of the three students sitting in emergency vehicles.

I sent my wife in the ambulance with Marcene. Our athletic director went with Estéban. And the security officers rode the bus home with the rest of the students. I walked to the police station and was able to get Carlos released quickly. They told him he would soon receive a call about the charges against him. We walked together to the hospital where Estéban was being cleared after a concussion check and Marcene was getting stitches in her lip. I was stepping in and out of her room as I made phone calls to parents. Each time, the parent on the other end of the line expressed nothing but relief that their child would be OK and that the situation was not more severe. At 2:30 a.m., all of the students were safely back in the care of their parents. I was shaken, frustrated, and frankly, angry.

The next night, we found ourselves playing for the state championship. We had no students in the stands to watch the game because we did not trust the police to treat our students properly if they returned. Although our team had not been in the incident the night before, they knew what had happened. We all wanted to win the trophy and take it home where we could celebrate safely and joyfully. We came from behind to win the game by six. It was the first basketball championship in our school's history!

Throughout the weekend, I thought about how our student body would react to what had happened. I knew that they would be upset, angry, and frustrated. They would certainly need to process what had happened. They would probably need some way to deal with their feelings. We had won the state championship, but we had also been treated with hostility and contempt by parents and students of another school and by the police. I knew that I had to be prepared to help our students deal with the events of that night.

I also wanted our students and their families to find some measure of justice, especially justice for the students who had been physically harmed and wrongly arrested. While planning a victory ceremony, I was also locating legal support for our students who were injured that night. I did not trust the police to treat them fairly if they returned with only their parents to seek redress. I found a nonprofit legal aid group that would help file complaints against the police and get Carlos's charges dropped. I wanted to help our students and their parents use the legal system to achieve remedy.

On Monday and throughout the week, to my surprise, our students acted as if our trouble after the game never happened. We decorated the halls and celebrated our victory with a Ceremony of Champions complete with resounding chants of "Ooh, aah, you shoulda been a Raptor!" It seemed that our encounter with a hostile crowd and with a hostile police force was par for the course.

During the weekend, I kept in touch with the families, checking on how the students were healing and processing the event. On Monday, I began to call parents to speak with them about filing complaints. I told them that I had lined up legal aid to support them. But, surprisingly, these parents turned down my offer of help. Their only interest was to make sure that Carlos would be cleared. All were adamant about fighting for him but not going any further. They said that they appreciated what I was trying to do, but they also signaled that there was something I didn't understand. One mother put it directly: "Why bother? We never win at these things."

I did file a complaint as a private citizen with the town's police department, believing that the officers that night needed to be held accountable for their actions. And charges against Carlos were dropped. We had won a state championship, and we were all grateful to walk away from the evening without any serious physical injury or arrests and police records. I could not help thinking that at the same time we came home winning, we also came home losing, accepting our experience as normal and seeing as futile efforts to seek justice through a system that is supposed to protect us all.

36. Summer Meals

Told by the director of a suburban community organization

As the director of a nonprofit community organization dedicated to addressing hunger and food insecurity across adjacent neighborhoods of a large city and its suburban ring, I had been concerned about the lack of access children in our service area had to meals in the summer. Across the country, of the kids who normally received free or reduced-price meals during the school year, only around 11 percent received them in the summer. It was not very different in our community.

Federal guidelines have been strict about who can provide summer meals to clients. The location of a summer meals distribution site is linked to the closest elementary school. If that school has less than a 40 percent poverty rate for students, a distribution site must require income verification for each student to be fed. Because the poverty rate of the elementary school nearest to our organization was consistently below this threshold, we had been unable to provide meals for students at our site. We believed that to require income verification for a drop-in meal program would not only be unfeasible but also potentially degrading to those who would benefit.

My staff and I approached the large local high school to see if it might, with our help, open its cafeteria during summer school, which would at least allow those students receiving free or reduced-priced food during the school year to have access to meals in the summer. About 20 percent of students at the high school were eligible for free or reduced-price meals—a total of about 800 kids. The school was unique in that it produced all school meals on site, and it served as the food vendor for one of its feeder districts of eight elementary and middle schools.

We first reached out to the director of food services and then to her boss, the director of finance. Citing staffing issues and budgetary concerns, neither was particularly enthusiastic

about the idea. I sought advice from a friend who is director of communications at the school, and she advised me to approach the school's associate principal for curriculum and instruction, who oversaw summer school and all the special summer school programs. I asked her to introduce us and pass along some information I had gathered on food insecurity and summer learning loss.

The associate principal and I met. He invited the school's coordinator of special summer programs to attend our meeting, and I brought along my summer meals coordinator. My coordinator had experience launching off-site summer meals programs with partners at qualifying schools in our larger service area. At the meeting, the school's summer programs coordinator let the associate principal know that she had been spending personal money on cheese sticks, yogurts, and granola bars to address this very problem.

We quickly came to recognize the need to provide summer meals and that we needed to find a way to make something work. The associate principal and summer programs coordinator suggested that we focus on students in one special summer program as a contained trial. This program served students who had struggled in eighth grade to make an effective transition to ninth grade. It was a 3½-hour daily program lasting 4 weeks, and it served nearly 40 students, most of whom were eligible for free or reduced-priced meals during the school year.

My summer meals coordinator and I agreed to hire an outside caterer to provide meals to these students so that high school staff would not need to be involved or paid. We agreed that all students in the program would be served to avoid stigma, and if the high school would certify which students were eligible for free and reduced-price meals, a good bit of the cost would be reduced. The school and my organization would split the cost of the meals for students who were not eligible for free and reduced-price meals. My organization would also provide the school with some logistical support.

The associate principal became a strong advocate for and assumed leadership of this initiative. He called the director of food services, who remained ambivalent. Pressing her a bit, he said that he would take responsibility for any audit or administrative issues. And he obtained the full support of the school's principal.

The meals program was launched in the eighth-to-ninth-grade transition program, and it provided lunches for all the students regardless of their eligibility for free or reduced-price meals. The kids ate each day. Inadvertently, an additional day of lunches was ordered. So, the school's summer program coordinator took the extra meals to students enrolled in another summer program at the school, a credit recovery program for students who had failed one or more classes the previous academic year. Her report: "The kids fell on them."

Later in the summer, the associate principal, the summer program coordinator, our staff, and I held a debriefing. The response was overwhelmingly positive. The associate principal asked us to work with the school to continue the meals program the following summer with the transition program and extend it to all the kids in the credit recovery program. He also wanted to include breakfast for all students in both programs. Because the number of meals and the funds to provide them would be large enough to involve the school's kitchen without a financial loss, we eliminated the outside caterer. Under the leadership of the associate principal, the school assumed responsibility for providing the meals in house. Our organization would continue to split the costs of meals for students not eligible for free and reduced-price lunches so that all could eat without stigma.

With high school administrative leadership paving the way, we approached the leadership of one of the high school's elementary and middle school feeder districts. We found a willing partner in the feeder district's new superintendent of curriculum, who had just left a principalship in another district that offered summer meals to free and reduced-price meal-eligible students. He was all for spearheading something similar in his new role. Learning of the success of the high school initiative and the support of the high school's administration, he thought working with us was a clear winner for all.

We quickly developed a plan to establish a summer meals program with shared responsibilities similar to the high school plan. But the elementary and middle school district's leadership decided that to be truly equitable, the meal program should not be piloted on a limited basis but rolled out completely for all students in all three of the district's summer programs, including those that promoted academic enrichment and that served students with disabilities and English language learners. This district further decided to begin by providing breakfast, with the possibility of expanding at a later date to also serving lunch. As with the high school, we agreed to split the costs of feeding students who were not eligible for free and reduce-price meals. The high school's leadership agreed to serve as the summer food vendor.

Our organization developed a parent and teacher survey to assess the success of this program. Parents were positive. And teachers were unanimous in their support. All teachers reported some positive impact on the kids, from improved behavior and fewer discipline issues to better ability to concentrate.

Like the high school, the elementary and middle school district expressed strong interest in continuing the programs over the long haul. Then COVID struck, and the programs were put on hiatus. Yet, because of the success of these efforts, leaders at both the high school and the feeder district began working with us to adapt to a grab-n-go model of food distribution so that kids could continue to eat even though the schools were closed and these summer programs were not being held in person.

37. Sharing the Peace

Told by an early childhood director at an urban PreK–12 Catholic school

Teachers are not made for COVID quarantine, especially preschool teachers. They are social creatures who thrive on interactions and love to give warm, fuzzy hugs and share feelings with their students. Our preschool teachers were doing their best to interact with their students with the technology they had, but they felt the physical and social disconnect that came with remote learning. Phone calls. Video chats. Interactive games. We all were making the best of our new reality.

Easter was around the corner. We had been teaching from home for a month. Everyone was feeling the first real losses of quarantine. Families could not gather for Easter picnics, and children couldn't attend an Easter egg hunt. Importantly, we couldn't attend Easter mass. As a Catholic school steeped in tradition, our inability to celebrate Easter brought an all-new realization that this virus was devastating to all facets of our lives. Our head of school must have felt our despair.

The week before Easter, I was gardening, a hobby I resurrected to keep myself occupied during quarantine. Out of nowhere my doorbell rang. It was a bit startling considering visitors were frowned upon during the safer-at-home era. When I went to the door, I was shocked to see my boss, the head of school. He was standing several feet away from my front porch in jeans and a T-shirt. He held a peace lily in his hand with a note attached. He simply said "Happy Easter" as he put it on my porch and walked away. I smiled and thanked him. As he drove away, tears started running down my face. What a kind gesture, what a beautiful flower, and what a pleasant surprise for my Sunday afternoon. I brought the flower in and immediately showed my family. My daughter and I started speculating how long it was going to take him to deliver Easter lilies to all 15 members of our leadership team. I imagined

he was logging quite a few miles in his pickup truck.

The next day, Monday, I hosted a Zoom faculty meeting with my early childhood teachers and their assistants. They seemed glum. They too were feeling the reality of our new situation. When I clicked "Leave" and it replied "End meeting for all," it hit me. I, too, could brighten their day, just like our school head did for our leadership team. I, too, could bring a little peace and joy to them this Easter.

I enlisted the help of my daughter, the local nursery, and Google maps. I plotted out the most efficient route to deliver flowers to my teachers and ordered 17 flowers, and my daughter made Easter bunny cards for each plant. We are preschool teachers after all! We estimated that it would take 4 hours to deliver the flowers to homes in nine different zip codes. After 2 days of preparation, my daughter and I headed off. I didn't call or text to say I was on the way. Everyone was home per health department regulations.

The first delivery was to one of our PreK teachers. She smiled but kept her distance. We talked for awhile about our new lives and the things we were doing to keep busy. She thanked me as I headed to the next house. Each delivery brought a bigger sense of happiness. I hadn't realized how much I missed these amazing women and that I needed this as much as they did. The day wore on. I hadn't accounted time for conversations into my plan, but it didn't matter how long it took. That day, my daughter and I made the rounds for 6 hours. Our last delivery was at 8:30 p.m. The door was answered by our after-school care receptionist's husband in his night robe. I was terribly embarrassed to be disturbing him, but he reassured me it was fine. We got home tired and fulfilled. The next day, Good Friday, we delivered the last two flowers. The last delivery was to our junior kindergarten assistant, who lived 40 minutes from my house. It was a long drive into the country, a peaceful drive that gave me time to count the blessings that each of these teachers brought to my life and to the lives of our students.

That Sunday was Easter. My family and I had an Easter egg hunt. We watched mass on television, ate our traditional Easter ham, and enjoyed our day. It was different than any other Easter, but it was filled with love, joy, and simple pleasures that I will always cherish.

Signs of Care—Annie Williamson, Grade 5

---

38. The Tsunami

Told by the former principal of an urban public high school

Going into my eighth year as principal, my colleagues and I took pride in our school's transformation from among the lowest 5 percent in the state to one of the best neighborhood high schools in the city. Through our hard work, our students' performance had improved dramatically. They knew that they had played a pivotal role in reclaiming their school by providing ideas for improvement, taking responsibility for the school, and their hard work. Our faculty had become deeply committed to a burgeoning professional culture marked by collaboration and by the development of caring, supportive relationships that promote *all* students' success in school. We began to be recognized for our work. We attracted money to provide students with scholarships for postsecondary education. We

won a state soccer championship. Our state's department of education awarded us a "commendable school" designation. And the *US News & World Report* placed us in the top third of high schools in the state.

The 2019–2020 school year started like other recent years with a day-long senior leadership retreat. Our agenda included typical items like a mission-focused data review and some collaborative problem-solving. Looking back at the agenda now, our closing activity stands out as an omen of sorts. It was titled "Self-Care and Sustainable Leadership," and it focused on strategies for self-care and avoiding compassion fatigue. Our team felt that we all needed new tools for the year ahead—teachers, staff, and school leaders alike. We had no idea what was coming—a tsunami of crises that would bring our school community to its knees.

The first wave hit early in the fall with a car accident that killed two of our seniors—sisters. They were vibrant popular young women who had gone out with an older sister on a school night. The night ended in the crash that also caused serious injuries to the older sister, who was driving. Most of our students learned about their classmates' deaths via social media as they walked into school the next day before we had the opportunity to craft the message and organize support for our students and teachers.

The second wave hit two days after the funeral for one of these students—a district-wide teachers strike that was to be the longest in more than three decades. It lasted 15 days. This strike felt different from the 7-day strike several years before. This one was especially disruptive. Our students were cut off from the crisis team and other supports that the school provided after the car accident. Instruction was cut off. Students who were eligible for free and reduced-price meals were left without food. And because of the timing of the strike, our athletes were not able to continue with fall sports. This was especially painful for our top-ranked boys soccer team that was favored to win another state championship.

The school community was still recovering from the accident and the strike when the next wave hit. During the third week of November, a former student, in his early 20s, was gang executed at a local convenience store. He had struggled academically as a student, but he was well-known within the school and the broader community. I had developed a friendship with his mother, who worked as a waitress in a nearby restaurant. We were all shocked when we heard the news, and we anticipated gang retribution. Two days later, a young man from the opposing gang, also a former student of ours, was executed, setting off 3 days of social media frenzy, fear, and additional neighborhood violence. Even though these events did not occur on school property

and no current students were involved, it was all but impossible to convince many parents that it was safe to send their children to school. Despite the fact that we had worked so hard to create a safe, trusting, and supportive school environment for students, attendance dropped below 50 percent for several days.

It was a tough fall, and the tsunami kept coming the next spring. A wave hit in early March when another one of our students lost her struggle with cancer. Our students and staff made efforts to honor her spirit and life before and after she passed away. Hers was our fifth death in 6 months.

Then COVID hit, and we lost our ability to be together in person. We were notified on Friday, March 13, that the governor would close schools across the state for 3 weeks. In fact, schools remained closed until the end of the academic year. Like most schools, we were not prepared. But we worked hard to adapt and transition to remote learning. We did our best to ensure that learning continued and that key rituals like graduation took place.

And still another wave came. In May, like in so many other places, our city experienced racial tensions and community unrest following the murder of George Floyd. For some students and staff, it was an opportunity to take to the streets and express anger and frustration over police brutality and lack of accountability. The violence and looting directly affected some of our families and their businesses. Life in parts of our neighborhoods was severely disrupted, compounding the loss and uncertainty that had been building for months.

As these waves hit us, we struggled against a strong, compounding cross current. The 2019–2020 school year was the final year of my second four-year contract. I knew going into the year that renewal was far from guaranteed. The political winds had shifted as our school's community-based governing council was beginning to feel like it was time to make a change, despite how well the school was performing. The council's politics had turned toxic, and by mid-fall, I began looking quietly for new positions while also working with council members to counter efforts that might harm the school. I began to feel like I was coming under steady attack even as the faculty and I continued our work with our students while managing the crises that hit us.

I took solace in family and friends and was grateful to feel God's love. It was a leadership coach at the time who remarked that in moments like these sometimes God calms the storm while in other moments God calms those who are in the storm. I was in the middle of the storm. At the end of January, the council decided not to offer me a third contract, terminating my principalship at the end of the school year. I accepted the council's decision, thanked the community for the opportunity to serve its families and children, and committed to a peaceful transition to new school leadership.

In the months that followed, I began to provide new leadership opportunities for my assistant principal and to help our council see that she was an excellent person to succeed me. She was highly skilled and respected by our faculty and staff, and she was our best hope to keep the school moving forward. I wanted to put her out front so that others could see her skills, her caring, and understand what a remarkable school leader she was. It worked. She applied for the job, and with some pressure from the staff and parents, the school council offered her a contract. I turned my attention to help her assume her new responsibilities. I felt assured that the school was going to be in good hands.

The 2019–2020 school year was a time of immense challenge for us and for our students and families. The year brought our school community to its knees. How did we make it through? In the end, we managed to come together around a vision rooted in a commitment to social justice and to being a caring and supportive community for all our students, teachers, and families. We had built a community that was bigger than any one of us and that would continue without me, with the leadership of the new school principal.

We grounded our school improvement work in student centeredness. We created a climate of access and opportunity for students, attending to social and structural barriers to student engagement and success. Importantly, as school leaders, we worked continually to help teachers form caring relationships with their students, to develop trust, and to provide social and emotional support. We helped teachers by adding professional staff who focused on behavioral and psychological health of students and by creating team structures to bring teachers together. It was the strength of this community of care and support that ultimately shifted our school to become more aligned to meet our students' needs and interests. We had become increasingly intentional in how we went about removing barriers and helping students feel like they belonged, were respected, and were supported. In the end, the school that we had built to be both challenging and caring would prevent us from drowning under these waves of crisis.

39. Leading Through the Storm

Told by the head of an urban K–12 independent Christian school

The first time leading a school into a new academic year is always challenging. You cannot be sure what to expect. As the new head of my K–12 independent school along the Gulf Coast, never did I imagine what the beginning of the 2017–2018 school year would bring—Hurricane Harvey, a Category 4 hurricane that devastated our city, including the bayou next to our campus.

Less than 2 months earlier, I had moved my wife and three children from the northeast to take this position. I expected to spend those first days of school greeting students and families as they returned to campus and getting to know my faculty and staff. Instead, I found myself leading a community through the most destructive storm in the history of the city.

The night before the storm, I hosted my first Back to School Night. News of a potential hurricane was on the screen of every phone, and the *big* question of the night was whether I would cancel school the next day, which I did after careful consideration. I did not anticipate the fury of the storm or that we would remain closed for 12 more days.

As the hurricane made landfall, school families evacuated their homes, fleeing to higher ground. Families who tried to stay were forced to leave in the middle of the night as water rose past the second floor of their homes. These midnight evacuations terrified many students, with some fearing the sound of running water for months later.

During the storm, my family and I evacuated to a town 3½ hours away. There, a friend and fellow head of school graciously gave me an office at his school. During my few days in evacuation, he provided valuable counsel to this newcomer as I began working through the challenges I knew would lie ahead.

I found myself heading a newly assembled leadership team whose members were also reeling from the hurricane. Many experienced significant flooding in their own homes and loss of property. Despite our personal challenges, my team sprang into action, calling each of our more than 200 school employees. We were constantly assessing the situation to determine the needs of our community and the priorities for each of us. We developed calling teams to contact each school family to assess their situations and to understand how each was personally affected. This launched us on a 10-day emergency mission to meet the expansive needs of everyone in our school community.

Despite the city-wide devastation, the storm had minimal impact on our school's campus. However, the homes of approximately 25 members of our faculty and staff and the homes of more than 50 school families were filled with water. Many of these families did not have flood insurance. Yet in the middle of this unfathomable damage and destruction, I saw God's hand at work through the members of this beloved community. One parent immediately rallied upper-school students to help families by cleaning out mud, water, and debris in homes that were flooded. Faculty members reached out to parents on email to make sure they and their children were safe. One of our alumni spent 36 straight hours rescuing families by boat as the waters rose. Our Parents Association organized a meal train to provide home-cooked meals to our families who could not get back into their homes. Several students and their families hosted classmates and families while they waited to find long-term housing. By the end of the first week following the storm, nearly 20,000 volunteers partnered with our school's church to clean more than 1,000 homes and distribute almost a half-million bottles of water. Harvey brought fear and destruction, but we found strength and courage in the promise and person of Christ.

As the water subsided, I walked into the home of one school family to see a mother devastated, unable to fully comprehend the damage to her home. I sat across from a father forced to evacuate his home by boat in the middle of the night with his wife, two children, and grandmother. As I helped families move furniture from their flooded homes to rental homes, I realized that caring for our community would require much more than food and lodging. Our students and their families were traumatized! Even those whose homes did not flood were affected by the destruction and loss all around them.

Because of the continuing challenges of flooding, street closures, and neighborhood evacuations, the date to resume school became a moving target. Together, my leadership team and I made the choice to be informative, intentional, and well defined in communicating with our school families. Our communications team was helpful in disseminating information through school emails and our emergency notification system.

Being informed, collaborating on decisions, and consistently communicating gave our families confidence in the school's leadership and helped ease some anxiety.

Returning to school was especially challenging. There were faculty and staff members dealing with devastating property loss. There were school families who lost everything. We needed our entire community to pitch in and remain flexible. We suspended our uniform dress code until we could provide replacement uniforms to students who had no uniforms to wear. Our faculty was flexible with students whose homes had no power or internet by modifying curricula and assignments. We postponed events and adapted school life to meet the needs of our battered and bruised community. The fallout from the storm affected us during the entire school year.

In my first faculty–staff address after Harvey, I offered encouragement with reminders of three core principles that define our school. The first is that God is in control. The second is that people are more important than possessions. And the third is that God has given us a great opportunity to be the hands and feet of Jesus. I asked the faculty and staff to continue to fill their tanks spiritually, emotionally, and physically. I reminded them that our most important job is first to care for the hearts and souls of our students and second to educate their minds.

When people go through a tragedy like this, we must work to understand what happened and how we can extend grace. Although we experienced Harvey as a community event, we also experienced it individually. Every family's story was different, and we each came out of it with different needs. It is critical to understand the individuality of each person and to extend grace in the immediate aftermath and throughout the recovery.

---

40. The Work of My Life

Told by the superintendent of a suburban K–8 public school district

Growing up I often thought that I would not live to see my adulthood. I did not have any vision of a future. I grew up in poverty, even though I never knew we were poor until I was much older. This was the way it was in my community. I grew up in a dysfunctional household without an adult male presence. My brothers and I did not have a clear idea of other possibilities. We often hoped our lives would come to an end so that we could be let out of our misery.

Somehow, I made it through high school and then college. After graduation, I still had no idea where I was heading or where I wanted to go. As I got older, I came to realize what I wanted to be. I knew I wanted to be a good father, a good man, and a difference maker. But I had no sense of calling, of vocation. I don't know how, but I became a teacher, a coach, a principal, and a superintendent. In fact, I served as the principal of two schools I attended as a student.

I entered these once-familiar worlds on the other side of the prism, looking out at the young faces wondering how I could make a difference to each and every one of them. As time passed, I became more invested in the lives of the students I served. I learned that these young people were like me, wondering if they would ever make it, whatever "it" meant, struggling to find their way without a sense of destination, not knowing how to get out of their challenging circumstances.

When I started my career, I did not understand what it meant to be a supportive and reflective leader. As a new teacher and coach, I got to know an eighth-grade student athlete. She was quiet, similar to me as an eighth grader, and she had a great deal of promise. I would often tell her that there were great things to come in her life. I tried to help her see a future out there. I thought I was making a difference. The school year continued, and our students were 3 weeks away from graduating and moving on to high school. She did not feel the same optimism as I did. Sadly, she committed suicide a few days short of her graduation. I was devastated. I thought I was making a difference in her life. I thought I could be the example for this young person. I thought I could let her know there was light at the end of the tunnel. I struggled through the rest of that school year and the next. I was uncertain about whether I could help. I fought doubts and insecurity and committed myself to try to make a difference in every student's life.

Soon I moved to another school and continued to share my experience with every student who reminded me of my former eighth-grade student–athlete. I wanted to let them know that they too can make a difference in the lives of others and that with perseverance things would get better, as they did for me. I learned that in addition to sharing my story and encouraging them to have hope in a bright future, I had to help students find ways to work concretely toward that future. It was not enough to be an example for them and to encourage them. I had to help them learn how to get there.

Unfortunately, far too many times I would lose my crusade. Too many of them died, some by suicide, many by violence in the community. In 20 years as a principal, I lost more than 30 students—far too many! Although this loss of life and the seemingly insurmountable challenges of poverty and violence shook my resolve at times, I continued my support of students and

If I'm Down—Elliott King, Grade 5

rededicated my efforts to find ways to empower them. I never gave up hope.

I remember Sam as one of the students who I was able to support through a difficult time of his life. Sam was a spongy little freshman, silent yet loud, and confident yet insecure. He was involved in everything we offered at the school. He was an active member of the speech and drama clubs. On some days, he would present himself as a leader among leaders. On other days, he was reserved and withdrawn.

As I got to know Sam, I began to see another side of him. Soon after the start of the second semester of his freshman year, I noticed Sam always wore long-sleeve shirts no matter the time of year. After talking with Sam, he revealed that he was masking his personal struggles by throwing himself into school activities. As we talked, I asked why he always covered his arms. After many conversations and building trust in our relationship, he revealed that he was self-mutilating, taking his pain out on his body,

trying to get the courage to end his life. Once I discovered Sam's secret, I worked hard to provide him the emotional support he needed. We formed a small community around him—his teachers, our counselors, and me. We built upon the relationship he and I had developed. I also began working with Human Services, which found a way for him to leave his dysfunctional and harmful family environment. Over time, the support we gave Sam helped him graduate from high school at the top of his class with honors. He had continued his involvement in school activities, and he had stopped self-mutilating. He had begun to display the true confidence we all recognized in him. Sam went on to attend a top-tier university.

We were able to help Sam see past his current existence and envision an alternative future. We were able to provide the care and support to help him get there. Far too many times my efforts did not end so well. But I keep trying. It is the work of my life.

Coda

A Culture of Caring

The stories in this book shine a bright light on the critical importance of caring in school leadership during times of crisis. They show how being caring of individuals and caring through school community can help schools encounter and recover from crisis. They tell of a wide range of emotional, psychological, and tangible benefits.

> Across these stories we see that caring in crisis situations is the same, at its heart, as caring during ordinary time. Its aims are the same. It flows from the same positive virtues and mindsets. And its enactment requires competence.

Across these stories we see that caring in crisis situations is the same, at its heart, as caring during ordinary times. Its aims are the same. It flows from the same positive virtues and mindsets. And its enactment requires competence. Crises may amplify the intensity of caring, and specific expressions may vary depending on the crisis situation. Nevertheless, we have no reason to believe that there are two models of caring leadership, one for ordinary times and one for times of crisis. Caring's expression across contexts are variations on the same themes.

These stories also remind us that even during crisis situations, caring is not something done apart from the core functions of school leadership. They emphasize that caring is best understood as a quality of school leadership during crisis, a quality of crisis leadership. As we wrote in the introduction, caring is the matter, the manner, and the motivation of leadership generally and in crisis leadership particularly. Caring school leaders do not engage in crisis leadership and caring leadership separately. It is of one piece.

We also recall from the introduction that caring is sometimes overlooked because of an assumption we make that caring is present and strong in schools because caring is what schools are supposed to do. This notion of "spontaneously occurring caring" is not always borne out. Indeed, the enactment and benefits of caring come to schools that do not take caring for granted but instead make caring a deliberate part of what they do and what they are. We see in a number

> Waiting for our better angels to emerge is not as efficacious a strategy to prepare for crisis as is systematically cultivating trusting, caring relationships that may not only prevent crises but will serve as a foundation for response and recovery.

of the stories that schools benefit immeasurably from the investments they make in cultivating positive social relationships and caring community *before* crises come. Crises may bring out the best in us, and they may prompt us to become more caring. But waiting for our better angels to emerge is not as efficacious a strategy to prepare for crisis as is systematically cultivating trusting, caring relationships that may not only prevent crises but will serve as a foundation for response and recovery.

It may be tempting to reduce the depth and breadth of caring once crises subside and students, teachers, and school leaders return to the regularities, busyness, and distractions of "normal" schooling. It may be tempting to take the foot off the gas. And it may be tempting to assume that the caring enacted during crisis will continue and that because we have been caring we will continue to be caring. There is real danger here, and we believe it would be a mistake to succumb to any of these temptations.

If crises bring out the best in us, if crises bring out the caring in us, there is no good reason to dial back or discontinue it when crises subside. Sir Winston Churchill is credited with first saying, "Never let a good crisis go to waste." If crisis brings out our better angels and we ignore or shoo them away as we reestablish some state of normalcy, we have let the opportunity to extend and strengthen caring go to waste. If good crisis leadership includes time for reflecting and learning, we might understand how important caring is to the success and well-being of all. We might decide to be as deliberate about caring after crisis as we were during crisis. And we might decide to pursue its benefits in the present and as a resource for the next crisis that comes.

Although its benefits are great, caring can be taxing. This is true during ordinary times, and it is especially true during crisis, when the need for caring and support becomes more acute. Caring in crisis can exact a tremendous personal toll.[78] It can lead to maladaptive behavior, errors in decision-making, physical exhaustion, and a sense of helplessness. Caring can result in compassion fatigue, the emotional overload that occurs when one gets overinvolved, overextended, and overwhelmed by the emotional, psychological, and physical demands imposed by others.[79] Indeed, caregivers can easily become "hidden victims" of crisis.[80] This problem is a common concern in professions that require constant work on behalf of others, where need is great, where crises arise frequently, and where situations are not conducive to caring or at least to the forms of caring to which we are accustomed. It is a problem vividly captured in the recent message, reprinted below, posted on LinkedIn by an elementary school principal in New Jersey. It is a problem conveyed in the words of a middle school principal who told us that during COVID, he was growing weary of "setting myself on fire to keep others warm."

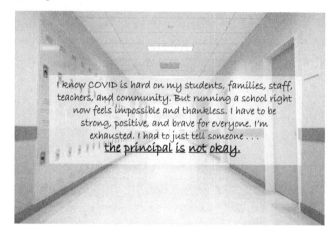

The Principal Is Not Okay—Tom Conroy, Elementary School Principal

Who Cares for the Caring School Leader?

To be truly caring of others, school leaders must also be cared for. A hospice chaplain made this point well when she spoke about her ministry as a service of care. She described herself and other human service providers as water pitchers. She compared her service and theirs to pouring water to quench the thirst of others; to comfort and heal them physically, emotionally, and spiritually; and to promote their well-being. She argued that to

> To serve others well . . . all who give care need to regularly replenish the water they pour. Without replenishment, they will run dry and be of little use to anyone.

---

[78] Pepper et al. (2010).
[79] Kinnic et al. (1996).
[80] Raphael (1986, p. 10).

serve others well, human service providers—indeed, all who give care—need to regularly replenish the water they pour. Without replenishment, they will run dry and be of little use to anyone.

So, who will be caring of the caring school leader? Where will the caring school leader find sources of replenishment? This question is important to ask during the regular course of school life. It is imperative to ask in times of crisis when the need, the caring work, and the stakes intensify.

School leaders are presumed to be the ones caring—of students, of teachers and staff, of families, of their school communities, even of the neighborhoods surrounding their schools. Yet, there is often little recognition of their need for care and support. Perhaps it is assumed that they have adequate sources of care readily available. But this is not necessarily true. It is not uncommon that central offices provide little support for school leaders, invest little in their professional learning and development, and often, inadvertently, make decisions that cause school leaders' work to become more complicated and difficult. Many districts do not lead with caring but instead with dehumanizing precepts associated with bureaucracy.

Such situations leave school leaders alone to put aside their need for caring, seek caring from other sources, or look for effective means of self-care. The latter has received substantial attention lately. Although self-care can be vitally important, too much emphasis on it can, ironically, place additional burden and stress on the school leader. It can also relieve central offices and other care providers of a professional, indeed, a moral duty to care. *Cura te ipsum*! Physician, heal thyself!

Sources of Care and Support for School Leaders

1. Family and friends

2. Clergy, clinicians, and other professional caregivers

3. Colleagues, students, and parents in the school community—indeed, the community of care that a caring school leader may cultivate for others

4. Formal and informal networks of school leaders

5. Central offices and boards

6. Leadership supervisors and coaches

7. Universities and other entities that prepare, develop, and support school leaders

8. Professional associations

Care and support of school leaders can come from many sources. It is safe to say that the school leaders' access to such sources varies widely. It is also safe to say that the quality and effectiveness of these sources vary. Many sources are available only through the self-initiating effort of the school leader or perhaps by the serendipity of time and place. It does not seem particularly caring, in crisis situations or in ordinary time, to make caring school leaders work to avail themselves of the care and support they may desperately need.

We raise the question "Who cares for the caring school leader?" not to answer it but to draw attention to it. We also raise the question as a challenge to central offices, boards, professional associations, and the profession at large. If we expect our school leaders to be caring of others, and if we expect school leaders to be particularly caring during times of crisis, we need to take seriously their need for care and support. If we do not, their pitchers will run dry. Students, teachers, staff, and families will not fully benefit from the care they can provide. And we will be derelict in our duty of care.

Bibliography

Anderson, L. (2018). Leadership during crisis: Navigating complexity and uncertainty. *Leader to Leader, (90)*, 49–54.

Argenti, P. (2020, Summer). Crisis communication: Lessons from 9/11. *Harvard Business Review* (Special Issue), 18–25.

Bauman, D. C. (2011). Evaluating ethical approaches to crisis leadership: Insights from unintentional harm research. *Journal of Business Ethics, 98*(2), 281–295.

Boin, A., Hart, P., Stern, E. J., & Sundelius, B. (2005). *The politics of crisis management: Public leadership under pressure.* New York, NY: Cambridge University Press.

Brechin, A. (1998). Introduction. In A. Brechin, J. Walmsley, J. Katz, & S. Peace (Eds.), *Care matters: Concepts, practice, and research in health and social care* (pp. 1–12). Thousand Oaks, CA: Sage.

Child Welfare League of America. (2020). Preschool children have a higher expulsion rates than K–12. https://www.cwla.org/preschool-children-have-a-higher-expulsion-rates-than-k-12/#:~:text=The%20research%20from%20a%20few,higher%20than%20three%2Dyear%20olds

Coles, R. (1989). *The call of stories: Teaching and the moral imagination.* Boston, MA: Houghton Mifflin.

Comfort, L. K. (2007). Crisis management in hindsight: Cognition, communication, coordination, and control. *Public Administration Review, 67*(s1), 189–197.

Donaldson, G. A. (2006). *Cultivating leadership in school: Connecting people, purpose, and practice.* New York, NY: Teachers College Press.

Dückers, M. L. A. (2017). A multilayered psychosocial resilience framework and its implications for community-focused crisis management. *Journal of Contingencies and Crisis Management, 25*(3), 182–187.

Engster, D. (2005). Rethinking care theory: The practice of caring and the obligation to care. *Hypatia, 20*(3), 50–74.

Flynn, T. (2002). *Crisis leadership: Learning from 9/11.* New York, NY: Counselors Academy, Public Relations Society of America.

Garmston, R. J. (2019). *The astonishing power of storytelling: Leading, teaching, and transforming in a new way.* Thousand Oaks, CA: Corwin.

Gigliotti, R. A. (2020). *Crisis leadership in higher education: Theory and practice.* New Brunswick, NJ: Rutgers University Press.

Heifetz, R., Grashow, A., & Linsky, M. (2020, Summer). Leadership in a (permanent) crisis. *Harvard Business Review* (Special Issue), pp. 11–17.

James, E. H., & Wooten, L. P. (2004). *Leadership in turbulent times: Competencies for thriving amidst crisis* (Working Paper Series No. 04-04). Charlottesville: University of Virginia, Darden Graduate School of Business Administration.

James, E. H., & Wooten, L. P. (2010). Orientations of positive leadership in times of crisis: In K. Cameron & G. Spreitzer (Eds.), *Handbook on positive organizational leadership* (pp. 882–894). New York, NY: Oxford University Press.

Kahn, L. H. (2020). *Who's in charge? Leadership during epidemics, bioterror attacks, and other public health crisis* (2nd ed.). Santa Barbara, CA: Praeger Security International.

Kerr, M. M., & King, G. (2019). *School crisis prevention and intervention* (2nd ed.). Long Grove, IL: Waveland Press.

Kinnic, K. N., Krugman, D. M., & Cameron, G. T. (1996). Compassion fatigue: Communication and burnout toward social problems. *Journalism and Mass Communication Quarterly, 73,* 687–707.

Klann, G. (2003). *Crisis leadership: Using military lessons, organizational experiences, and the power of influence to lessen the impact of chaos on the people you lead.* Greensboro, NC: Center for Creative Leadership.

Koehn, N. (2020). Real leaders are forged in crisis. In *Coronavirus: Leadership and recovery* (pp. 25–35). Boston, MA: Harvard Business Review Press.

MacNeil, W., & Topping, K. (2007). Crisis management in schools: Evidence-based prevention. *Journal of Educational Enquiry, 7*(1), 64–94.

Mintzberg, H. (2019). *Bedtime stories for managers.* Oakland, CA: Berrett-Kohler.

Mitroff, I. I., Pauchant, T. C., & Shrivastava, P. (1988). The structure of man-made organizational crises: Conceptual and empirical issues in the development of a general theory of crisis management. *Technological Forecasting and Social Change, 33*(2), 83–107.

Mitroff, I. I., Shrivastava, P., & Udwadia, F. E. (1987). Effective crisis management. *Academic of Management Executive, 1*(3), 283–292.

Mutch, C. (2015). Leadership in times of crisis: Dispositional, relational and contextual factors influencing school principals' actions. *International Journal of Disaster Risk Reduction, 14*(2), 186–194.

Noddings, N. (2013). *Caring: A relational approach to ethics and moral education* (2nd ed.). Berkeley: University of California Press.

O'Connor, P., & Takahashi, N. (2014). From caring about to caring for: Case studies of New Zealand and Japanese schools post disaster. *Pastoral Care in Education, 32*(10), 42–53.

Pearson, C. M., Clair, J. A., Misra, S. K., & Mitroff, I. I. (1997). Managing the unthinkable. *Organizational Dynamics, 26*(2), 51–64.

Pearson, C. M., & Mitroff, I. I. (1993). From crisis prone to crisis prepared: A framework for crisis management. *Academic of Management Executive, 7*(1), 48–59.

Pepper, M. J., London, T. D., Dishman, M. L., & Lewis, J. L. (2010). *Leading schools during crisis: What school administrators must know.* Lanham, MD: Rowman & Littlefield.

Quarantelli, E. L. (1998). Disaster crisis management: A summary of research findings. *Journal of Management Studies, 25*(4), 373–385.

Raphael, B. (1986). *When disaster strikes: How individuals and communities cope with catastrophe.* New York, NY: Basic Books.

Schein, E. H. (2013). *Humble inquiry: The gentle art of asking instead of telling.* San Francisco, CA: Berrett-Koehler.

Sharfstein, J. M. (2018). *The public health crisis survival guide: Leadership and management in trying times.* New York, NY: Oxford University Press.

Smylie, M. A., Murphy, J., & Louis, K. S. (2020). *Caring school leadership.* Thousand Oaks, CA: Corwin.

Smylie, M. A., Murphy, J., & Louis, K. S. (2021). *Stories of caring school leadership.* Thousand Oaks, CA: Corwin.

Sutton, R. I. (2020, Summer). How to be a good boss in a bad economy. *Harvard Business Review* (Special Issue), pp. 83–89.

Tate, J. S., & Dunklee, D. R. (2005). *Strategic listening for school leaders.* Thousand Oaks, CA: Corwin.

Teo, W. L., Lee, M., & Lim, W.-S. (2017). The relational activation of resilience model: How leadership activates resilience in an organizational crisis. *Journal of Contingencies and Crisis Management, 25*(3), 136–147.

Thompson, R. A. (2004). *Crisis intervention and crisis management: Strategies that work in schools and communities.* New York, NY: Routledge.

Tronto, J. C. (2005). An ethic of care. In A. D. Cudd & R. O. Andreasen (Eds.), *Feminist theory: A philosophical anthology* (pp. 251–263). Malden, MA: Blackwell.

Waldron, T., & Wetherbe, J. (2020). Ensure that your customer relationships outlast coronavirus. In *Coronavirus: Leadership and recovery* (pp. 113–122). Boston, MA: Harvard Business Review Press.

Leadership That Makes an Impact

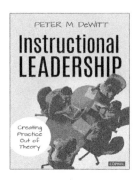

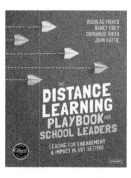

PETER M. DEWITT

This step-by-step how-to guide presents the six driving forces of instructional leadership within a multistage model for implementation, delivering lasting improvement through small collaborative changes.

JOHN HATTIE & RAYMOND L. SMITH

Based on the most current Visible Learning® research with contributions from education thought leaders around the world, this book includes practical ideas for leaders to implement high-impact strategies to strengthen entire school cultures and advocate for all students.

DOUGLAS FISHER, NANCY FREY, DOMINIQUE SMITH, & JOHN HATTIE

This essential hands-on resource offers guidance on leading school and school systems from a distance and delivering on the promise of equitable, quality learning experiences for students.

STEVEN M. CONSTANTINO

Explore the how-to's of establishing family empowerment through building trust, and reflect on implicit bias, equitable learning outcomes, and the role family engagement plays.

MICHAEL FULLAN, JOANNE QUINN, & JOANNE MCEACHEN

The comprehensive strategy of deep learning incorporates practical tools and processes to engage educational stakeholders in new partnerships, mobilize whole-system change, and transform learning for all students.

JOANNE QUINN, JOANNE MCEACHEN, MICHAEL FULLAN, MAG GARDNER, & MAX DRUMMY

Dive into deep learning with this hands-on guide to creating learning experiences that give purpose, unleash student potential, and transform not only learning, but life itself.

DAVIS CAMPBELL & MICHAEL FULLAN

The model outlined in this book develops a systems approach to governing local schools collaboratively to become exemplars of highly effective decision making, leadership, and action.

DAVIS CAMPBELL, MICHAEL FULLAN, BABS KAVANAUGH, & ELEANOR ADAM

As a supplement to the best-selling *The Governance Core*, this guide will help trustees and superintendents adopt a governance mindset and cohesive partnership.

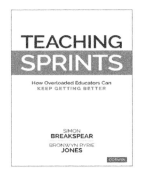

**SIMON BREAKSPEAR &
BRONWYN RYRIE JONES**

Realistic in demand and innovative in approach, this practical and powerful improvement process is designed to help all teachers get going, and keep going, with incremental professional improvement in schools.

**JAMES BAILEY &
RANDY WEINER**

The thought-provoking daily reflections in this guided journal are designed to strengthen the social and emotional skills of leaders and create a strong social-emotional environment for leaders, teachers, and students.

**MARK WHITE &
DWIGHT L. CARTER**

Through understanding the past and envisioning the future, the authors use practical exercises and real-life examples to draw the blueprint for adapting schools to the age of hyper-change.

**ALLAN G. OSBORNE, JR.
& CHARLES J. RUSSO**

With its user-friendly format, this resource will help educators understand the law so they can focus on providing exemplary education to students.

**MICHAEL FULLAN &
MARY JEAN GALLAGHER**

With the goal of transforming the culture of learning to develop greater equity, excellence, and student well-being, this book will help you liberate the system and maintain focus.

**TOM VANDER ARK
& EMILY LIEBTAG**

Diverse case studies and a framework based on timely issues help educators focus students' talents and interests on developing an entrepreneurial mindset and leadership skills.

THOMAS HATCH

By highlighting what works and demonstrating what can be accomplished if we redefine conventional schools, we can have more efficient, more effective, and more equitable schools and create powerful opportunities to support all aspects of students' development.

LYN SHARRATT

Explore 14 essential parameters to guide system and school leaders toward building powerful collaborative learning cultures.

CORWIN

CORWIN
A SAGE Publishing Company

Helping educators make the greatest impact

CORWIN HAS ONE MISSION: to enhance education through intentional professional learning.

We build long-term relationships with our authors, educators, clients, and associations who partner with us to develop and continuously improve the best evidence-based practices that establish and support lifelong learning.

Printed in Great Britain
by Amazon

74654508R00072